Are we nearly there yet?

'*How many*', type games your children can play in your car, when in a long journey.

100 pages for 100 journeys of peace and quiet!
6" x 9"

Who is in car?

____

____

____

Car colours:	Red □ Blue □ Green □ Yellow □
	Black □ White □ Silver □ Other □
Coaches?	1 □ 10 □ 20 □ 30 □ 40 □ 50 □ More □
Lorries?	1 □ 10 □ 20 □ 30 □ 40 □ 50 □ More □
Motor Bikes?	1 □ 10 □ 20 □ 30 □ 40 □ 50 □ More □
Caravans?	
Police Cars?	1 □ 2 □ 3 □ 4 □ 5 □ 10 □ More □
Cows?	1 □ 5 □ 10 □ 15 □ 20 □ 30 □ More □
Sheep?	1 □ 5 □ 10 □ 15 □ 20 □ 30 □ More □
Horses?	1 □ 5 □ 10 □ 15 □ 20 □ 30 □ More □
Windmills?	1 □ 2 □ 3 □ 4 □ 5 □ 10 □ More □
Trains?	1 □ 2 □ 3 □ 4 □ 5 □ 10 □ More □
Planes?	1 □ 2 □ 3 □ 4 □ 5 □ 10 □ More □
Who saw the first service station?	_______________________
Who saw the sea first?	_______________________
First asking to pee?	_______________________
First to say I'm hungry?	_______________________
First to say I'm thirsty?	_______________________
First to say *"Are we nearly there yet?"*	_______________________
Winner of dead lions?	_______________________

Who is in car? ______________________________
____
____

Car colours:	Red □ Blue □ Green □ Yellow □
	Black □ White □ Silver □ Other □
Coaches?	1 □ 10 □ 20 □ 30 □ 40 □ 50 □ More □
Lorries?	1 □ 10 □ 20 □ 30 □ 40 □ 50 □ More □
Motor Bikes?	1 □ 10 □ 20 □ 30 □ 40 □ 50 □ More □
Caravans?	
Police Cars?	1 □ 2 □ 3 □ 4 □ 5 □ 10 □ More □
Cows?	1 □ 5 □ 10 □ 15 □ 20 □ 30 □ More □
Sheep?	1 □ 5 □ 10 □ 15 □ 20 □ 30 □ More □
Horses?	1 □ 5 □ 10 □ 15 □ 20 □ 30 □ More □
Windmills?	1 □ 2 □ 3 □ 4 □ 5 □ 10 □ More □
Trains?	1 □ 2 □ 3 □ 4 □ 5 □ 10 □ More □
Planes?	1 □ 2 □ 3 □ 4 □ 5 □ 10 □ More □
Who saw the first service station?	_______________________
Who saw the sea first?	_______________________
First asking to pee?	_______________________
First to say I'm hungry?	_______________________
First to say I'm thirsty?	_______________________
First to say *"Are we nearly there yet?"*	_______________________
Winner of dead lions?	_______________________

Who is in car? ______________________________
____
____

Car colours:	Red □ Blue □ Green □ Yellow □
	Black □ White □ Silver □ Other □
Coaches?	1 □ 10 □ 20 □ 30 □ 40 □ 50 □ More □
Lorries?	1 □ 10 □ 20 □ 30 □ 40 □ 50 □ More □
Motor Bikes?	1 □ 10 □ 20 □ 30 □ 40 □ 50 □ More □
Caravans?	
Police Cars?	1 □ 2 □ 3 □ 4 □ 5 □ 10 □ More □
Cows?	1 □ 5 □ 10 □ 15 □ 20 □ 30 □ More □
Sheep?	1 □ 5 □ 10 □ 15 □ 20 □ 30 □ More □
Horses?	1 □ 5 □ 10 □ 15 □ 20 □ 30 □ More □
Windmills?	1 □ 2 □ 3 □ 4 □ 5 □ 10 □ More □
Trains?	1 □ 2 □ 3 □ 4 □ 5 □ 10 □ More □
Planes?	1 □ 2 □ 3 □ 4 □ 5 □ 10 □ More □
Who saw the first service station?	__________________________
Who saw the sea first?	__________________________
First asking to pee?	__________________________
First to say I'm hungry?	__________________________
First to say I'm thirsty?	__________________________
First to say *"Are we nearly there yet?"*	__________________________
Winner of dead lions?	__________________________

<table>
<tr><td>

Who is in car?

</td><td>

____

____

____

</td></tr>
</table>

Car colours:	Red □ Blue □ Green □ Yellow □
	Black □ White □ Silver □ Other □
Coaches?	1 □ 10 □ 20 □ 30 □ 40 □ 50 □ More □
Lorries?	1 □ 10 □ 20 □ 30 □ 40 □ 50 □ More □
Motor Bikes?	1 □ 10 □ 20 □ 30 □ 40 □ 50 □ More □
Caravans?	
Police Cars?	1 □ 2 □ 3 □ 4 □ 5 □ 10 □ More □
Cows?	1 □ 5 □ 10 □ 15 □ 20 □ 30 □ More □
Sheep?	1 □ 5 □ 10 □ 15 □ 20 □ 30 □ More □
Horses?	1 □ 5 □ 10 □ 15 □ 20 □ 30 □ More □
Windmills?	1 □ 2 □ 3 □ 4 □ 5 □ 10 □ More □
Trains?	1 □ 2 □ 3 □ 4 □ 5 □ 10 □ More □
Planes?	1 □ 2 □ 3 □ 4 □ 5 □ 10 □ More □
Who saw the first service station?	_______________________________
Who saw the sea first?	_______________________________
First asking to pee?	_______________________________
First to say I'm hungry?	_______________________________
First to say I'm thirsty?	_______________________________
First to say *"Are we nearly there yet?"*	_______________________________
Winner of dead lions?	_______________________________

Who is in car? ___________________
____
____

Car colours:	Red ☐ Blue ☐ Green ☐ Yellow ☐
	Black ☐ White ☐ Silver ☐ Other ☐
Coaches?	1 ☐ 10 ☐ 20 ☐ 30 ☐ 40 ☐ 50 ☐ More ☐
Lorries?	1 ☐ 10 ☐ 20 ☐ 30 ☐ 40 ☐ 50 ☐ More ☐
Motor Bikes?	1 ☐ 10 ☐ 20 ☐ 30 ☐ 40 ☐ 50 ☐ More ☐
Caravans?	
Police Cars?	1 ☐ 2 ☐ 3 ☐ 4 ☐ 5 ☐ 10 ☐ More ☐
Cows?	1 ☐ 5 ☐ 10 ☐ 15 ☐ 20 ☐ 30 ☐ More ☐
Sheep?	1 ☐ 5 ☐ 10 ☐ 15 ☐ 20 ☐ 30 ☐ More ☐
Horses?	1 ☐ 5 ☐ 10 ☐ 15 ☐ 20 ☐ 30 ☐ More ☐
Windmills?	1 ☐ 2 ☐ 3 ☐ 4 ☐ 5 ☐ 10 ☐ More ☐
Trains?	1 ☐ 2 ☐ 3 ☐ 4 ☐ 5 ☐ 10 ☐ More ☐
Planes?	1 ☐ 2 ☐ 3 ☐ 4 ☐ 5 ☐ 10 ☐ More ☐
Who saw the first service station?	_______________________
Who saw the sea first?	_______________________
First asking to pee?	_______________________
First to say I'm hungry?	_______________________
First to say I'm thirsty?	_______________________
First to say *"Are we nearly there yet?"*	_______________________
Winner of dead lions?	_______________________

Who is in car? _______________________________

____

____

Car colours:	Red □ Blue □ Green □ Yellow □
	Black □ White □ Silver □ Other □
Coaches?	1 □ 10 □ 20 □ 30 □ 40 □ 50 □ More □
Lorries?	1 □ 10 □ 20 □ 30 □ 40 □ 50 □ More □
Motor Bikes?	1 □ 10 □ 20 □ 30 □ 40 □ 50 □ More □
Caravans?	
Police Cars?	1 □ 2 □ 3 □ 4 □ 5 □ 10 □ More □
Cows?	1 □ 5 □ 10 □ 15 □ 20 □ 30 □ More □
Sheep?	1 □ 5 □ 10 □ 15 □ 20 □ 30 □ More □
Horses?	1 □ 5 □ 10 □ 15 □ 20 □ 30 □ More □
Windmills?	1 □ 2 □ 3 □ 4 □ 5 □ 10 □ More □
Trains?	1 □ 2 □ 3 □ 4 □ 5 □ 10 □ More □
Planes?	1 □ 2 □ 3 □ 4 □ 5 □ 10 □ More □

Who saw the first service station? _______________________________

Who saw the sea first? _______________________________

First asking to pee? _______________________________

First to say I'm hungry? _______________________________

First to say I'm thirsty? _______________________________

First to say *"Are we nearly there yet?"* _______________________________

Winner of dead lions? _______________________________

Who is in car? ______________________________
____
____

Car colours:	Red □ Blue □ Green □ Yellow □
	Black □ White □ Silver □ Other □
Coaches?	1 □ 10 □ 20 □ 30 □ 40 □ 50 □ More □
Lorries?	1 □ 10 □ 20 □ 30 □ 40 □ 50 □ More □
Motor Bikes?	1 □ 10 □ 20 □ 30 □ 40 □ 50 □ More □
Caravans?	
Police Cars?	1 □ 2 □ 3 □ 4 □ 5 □ 10 □ More □
Cows?	1 □ 5 □ 10 □ 15 □ 20 □ 30 □ More □
Sheep?	1 □ 5 □ 10 □ 15 □ 20 □ 30 □ More □
Horses?	1 □ 5 □ 10 □ 15 □ 20 □ 30 □ More □
Windmills?	1 □ 2 □ 3 □ 4 □ 5 □ 10 □ More □
Trains?	1 □ 2 □ 3 □ 4 □ 5 □ 10 □ More □
Planes?	1 □ 2 □ 3 □ 4 □ 5 □ 10 □ More □
Who saw the first service station?	______________________________
Who saw the sea first?	______________________________
First asking to pee?	______________________________
First to say I'm hungry?	______________________________
First to say I'm thirsty?	______________________________
First to say *"Are we nearly there yet?"*	______________________________
Winner of dead lions?	______________________________

Who is in car?

____

____

____

Car colours:	Red □ Blue □ Green □ Yellow □
	Black □ White □ Silver □ Other □
Coaches?	1 □ 10 □ 20 □ 30 □ 40 □ 50 □ More □
Lorries?	1 □ 10 □ 20 □ 30 □ 40 □ 50 □ More □
Motor Bikes?	1 □ 10 □ 20 □ 30 □ 40 □ 50 □ More □
Caravans?	
Police Cars?	1 □ 2 □ 3 □ 4 □ 5 □ 10 □ More □
Cows?	1 □ 5 □ 10 □ 15 □ 20 □ 30 □ More □
Sheep?	1 □ 5 □ 10 □ 15 □ 20 □ 30 □ More □
Horses?	1 □ 5 □ 10 □ 15 □ 20 □ 30 □ More □
Windmills?	1 □ 2 □ 3 □ 4 □ 5 □ 10 □ More □
Trains?	1 □ 2 □ 3 □ 4 □ 5 □ 10 □ More □
Planes?	1 □ 2 □ 3 □ 4 □ 5 □ 10 □ More □

Who saw the first service station? __________________________

Who saw the sea first? __________________________

First asking to pee? __________________________

First to say I'm hungry? __________________________

First to say I'm thirsty? __________________________

First to say *"Are we nearly there yet?"* __________________________

Winner of dead lions? __________________________

Who is in car?

____

____

____

Car colours:	Red □ Blue □ Green □ Yellow □
	Black □ White □ Silver □ Other □
Coaches?	1 □ 10 □ 20 □ 30 □ 40 □ 50 □ More □
Lorries?	1 □ 10 □ 20 □ 30 □ 40 □ 50 □ More □
Motor Bikes?	1 □ 10 □ 20 □ 30 □ 40 □ 50 □ More □
Caravans?	
Police Cars?	1 □ 2 □ 3 □ 4 □ 5 □ 10 □ More □
Cows?	1 □ 5 □ 10 □ 15 □ 20 □ 30 □ More □
Sheep?	1 □ 5 □ 10 □ 15 □ 20 □ 30 □ More □
Horses?	1 □ 5 □ 10 □ 15 □ 20 □ 30 □ More □
Windmills?	1 □ 2 □ 3 □ 4 □ 5 □ 10 □ More □
Trains?	1 □ 2 □ 3 □ 4 □ 5 □ 10 □ More □
Planes?	1 □ 2 □ 3 □ 4 □ 5 □ 10 □ More □

Who saw the first service station? _______________________________

Who saw the sea first? _______________________________

First asking to pee? _______________________________

First to say I'm hungry? _______________________________

First to say I'm thirsty? _______________________________

First to say *"Are we nearly there yet?"* _______________________________

Winner of dead lions? _______________________________

Who is in car?

____

____

____

Car colours:	Red □ Blue □ Green □ Yellow □
	Black □ White □ Silver □ Other □
Coaches?	1 □ 10 □ 20 □ 30 □ 40 □ 50 □ More □
Lorries?	1 □ 10 □ 20 □ 30 □ 40 □ 50 □ More □
Motor Bikes?	1 □ 10 □ 20 □ 30 □ 40 □ 50 □ More □
Caravans?	
Police Cars?	1 □ 2 □ 3 □ 4 □ 5 □ 10 □ More □
Cows?	1 □ 5 □ 10 □ 15 □ 20 □ 30 □ More □
Sheep?	1 □ 5 □ 10 □ 15 □ 20 □ 30 □ More □
Horses?	1 □ 5 □ 10 □ 15 □ 20 □ 30 □ More □
Windmills?	1 □ 2 □ 3 □ 4 □ 5 □ 10 □ More □
Trains?	1 □ 2 □ 3 □ 4 □ 5 □ 10 □ More □
Planes?	1 □ 2 □ 3 □ 4 □ 5 □ 10 □ More □

Who saw the first service station? ______________________________

Who saw the sea first? ______________________________

First asking to pee? ______________________________

First to say I'm hungry? ______________________________

First to say I'm thirsty? ______________________________

First to say *"Are we nearly there yet?"* ______________________________

Winner of dead lions? ______________________________

Who is in car?

____
____
____

Car colours:	Red □ Blue □ Green □ Yellow □ Black □ White □ Silver □ Other □
Coaches?	1 □ 10 □ 20 □ 30 □ 40 □ 50 □ More □
Lorries?	1 □ 10 □ 20 □ 30 □ 40 □ 50 □ More □
Motor Bikes?	1 □ 10 □ 20 □ 30 □ 40 □ 50 □ More □
Caravans?	
Police Cars?	1 □ 2 □ 3 □ 4 □ 5 □ 10 □ More □
Cows?	1 □ 5 □ 10 □ 15 □ 20 □ 30 □ More □
Sheep?	1 □ 5 □ 10 □ 15 □ 20 □ 30 □ More □
Horses?	1 □ 5 □ 10 □ 15 □ 20 □ 30 □ More □
Windmills?	1 □ 2 □ 3 □ 4 □ 5 □ 10 □ More □
Trains?	1 □ 2 □ 3 □ 4 □ 5 □ 10 □ More □
Planes?	1 □ 2 □ 3 □ 4 □ 5 □ 10 □ More □
Who saw the first service station?	______________________________
Who saw the sea first?	______________________________
First asking to pee?	______________________________
First to say I'm hungry?	______________________________
First to say I'm thirsty?	______________________________
First to say *"Are we nearly there yet?"*	______________________________
Winner of dead lions?	______________________________

Who is in car?

____

____

____

Car colours: Red □ Blue □ Green □ Yellow □

                           Black □ White □ Silver □ Other □

Coaches?   1 □ 10 □ 20 □ 30 □ 40 □ 50 □ More □

Lorries?   1 □ 10 □ 20 □ 30 □ 40 □ 50 □ More □

Motor Bikes?   1 □ 10 □ 20 □ 30 □ 40 □ 50 □ More □

Caravans?

Police Cars?   1 □ 2 □ 3 □ 4 □ 5 □ 10 □ More □

Cows?   1 □ 5 □ 10 □ 15 □ 20 □ 30 □ More □

Sheep?   1 □ 5 □ 10 □ 15 □ 20 □ 30 □ More □

Horses?   1 □ 5 □ 10 □ 15 □ 20 □ 30 □ More □

Windmills?   1 □ 2 □ 3 □ 4 □ 5 □ 10 □ More □

Trains?   1 □ 2 □ 3 □ 4 □ 5 □ 10 □ More □

Planes?   1 □ 2 □ 3 □ 4 □ 5 □ 10 □ More □

Who saw the first service station?   _______________________________

Who saw the sea first?   _______________________________

First asking to pee?   _______________________________

First to say I'm hungry?   _______________________________

First to say I'm thirsty?   _______________________________

First to say *"Are we nearly there yet?"*   _______________________________

Winner of dead lions?   _______________________________

Who is in car?

____

____

____

Car colours:	Red □ Blue □ Green □ Yellow □
	Black □ White □ Silver □ Other □
Coaches?	1 □ 10 □ 20 □ 30 □ 40 □ 50 □ More □
Lorries?	1 □ 10 □ 20 □ 30 □ 40 □ 50 □ More □
Motor Bikes?	1 □ 10 □ 20 □ 30 □ 40 □ 50 □ More □
Caravans?	
Police Cars?	1 □ 2 □ 3 □ 4 □ 5 □ 10 □ More □
Cows?	1 □ 5 □ 10 □ 15 □ 20 □ 30 □ More □
Sheep?	1 □ 5 □ 10 □ 15 □ 20 □ 30 □ More □
Horses?	1 □ 5 □ 10 □ 15 □ 20 □ 30 □ More □
Windmills?	1 □ 2 □ 3 □ 4 □ 5 □ 10 □ More □
Trains?	1 □ 2 □ 3 □ 4 □ 5 □ 10 □ More □
Planes?	1 □ 2 □ 3 □ 4 □ 5 □ 10 □ More □

Who saw the first service station? _______________________________

Who saw the sea first? _______________________________

First asking to pee? _______________________________

First to say I'm hungry? _______________________________

First to say I'm thirsty? _______________________________

First to say *"Are we nearly there yet?"* _______________________________

Winner of dead lions? _______________________________

Who is in car?

____
____
____

Car colours:	Red □ Blue □ Green □ Yellow □
	Black □ White □ Silver □ Other □
Coaches?	1 □ 10 □ 20 □ 30 □ 40 □ 50 □ More □
Lorries?	1 □ 10 □ 20 □ 30 □ 40 □ 50 □ More □
Motor Bikes?	1 □ 10 □ 20 □ 30 □ 40 □ 50 □ More □
Caravans?	
Police Cars?	1 □ 2 □ 3 □ 4 □ 5 □ 10 □ More □
Cows?	1 □ 5 □ 10 □ 15 □ 20 □ 30 □ More □
Sheep?	1 □ 5 □ 10 □ 15 □ 20 □ 30 □ More □
Horses?	1 □ 5 □ 10 □ 15 □ 20 □ 30 □ More □
Windmills?	1 □ 2 □ 3 □ 4 □ 5 □ 10 □ More □
Trains?	1 □ 2 □ 3 □ 4 □ 5 □ 10 □ More □
Planes?	1 □ 2 □ 3 □ 4 □ 5 □ 10 □ More □
Who saw the first service station?	_____________________
Who saw the sea first?	_____________________
First asking to pee?	_____________________
First to say I'm hungry?	_____________________
First to say I'm thirsty?	_____________________
First to say _"Are we nearly there yet?"_	_____________________
Winner of dead lions?	_____________________

Who is in car?

____

____

____

Car colours:	Red □ Blue □ Green □ Yellow □
	Black □ White □ Silver □ Other □
Coaches?	1 □ 10 □ 20 □ 30 □ 40 □ 50 □ More □
Lorries?	1 □ 10 □ 20 □ 30 □ 40 □ 50 □ More □
Motor Bikes?	1 □ 10 □ 20 □ 30 □ 40 □ 50 □ More □
Caravans?	
Police Cars?	1 □ 2 □ 3 □ 4 □ 5 □ 10 □ More □
Cows?	1 □ 5 □ 10 □ 15 □ 20 □ 30 □ More □
Sheep?	1 □ 5 □ 10 □ 15 □ 20 □ 30 □ More □
Horses?	1 □ 5 □ 10 □ 15 □ 20 □ 30 □ More □
Windmills?	1 □ 2 □ 3 □ 4 □ 5 □ 10 □ More □
Trains?	1 □ 2 □ 3 □ 4 □ 5 □ 10 □ More □
Planes?	1 □ 2 □ 3 □ 4 □ 5 □ 10 □ More □
Who saw the first service station?	___________________
Who saw the sea first?	___________________
First asking to pee?	___________________
First to say I'm hungry?	___________________
First to say I'm thirsty?	___________________
First to say *"Are we nearly there yet?"*	___________________
Winner of dead lions?	___________________

Who is in car? _______________________

____

____

Car colours:	Red □ Blue □ Green □ Yellow □
	Black □ White □ Silver □ Other □
Coaches?	1 □ 10 □ 20 □ 30 □ 40 □ 50 □ More □
Lorries?	1 □ 10 □ 20 □ 30 □ 40 □ 50 □ More □
Motor Bikes?	1 □ 10 □ 20 □ 30 □ 40 □ 50 □ More □
Caravans?	
Police Cars?	1 □ 2 □ 3 □ 4 □ 5 □ 10 □ More □
Cows?	1 □ 5 □ 10 □ 15 □ 20 □ 30 □ More □
Sheep?	1 □ 5 □ 10 □ 15 □ 20 □ 30 □ More □
Horses?	1 □ 5 □ 10 □ 15 □ 20 □ 30 □ More □
Windmills?	1 □ 2 □ 3 □ 4 □ 5 □ 10 □ More □
Trains?	1 □ 2 □ 3 □ 4 □ 5 □ 10 □ More □
Planes?	1 □ 2 □ 3 □ 4 □ 5 □ 10 □ More □
Who saw the first service station?	_______________________
Who saw the sea first?	_______________________
First asking to pee?	_______________________
First to say I'm hungry?	_______________________
First to say I'm thirsty?	_______________________
First to say *"Are we nearly there yet?"*	_______________________
Winner of dead lions?	_______________________

Who is in car?

____

____

____

Car colours:	Red □ Blue □ Green □ Yellow □
	Black □ White □ Silver □ Other □
Coaches?	1 □ 10 □ 20 □ 30 □ 40 □ 50 □ More □
Lorries?	1 □ 10 □ 20 □ 30 □ 40 □ 50 □ More □
Motor Bikes?	1 □ 10 □ 20 □ 30 □ 40 □ 50 □ More □
Caravans?	
Police Cars?	1 □ 2 □ 3 □ 4 □ 5 □ 10 □ More □
Cows?	1 □ 5 □ 10 □ 15 □ 20 □ 30 □ More □
Sheep?	1 □ 5 □ 10 □ 15 □ 20 □ 30 □ More □
Horses?	1 □ 5 □ 10 □ 15 □ 20 □ 30 □ More □
Windmills?	1 □ 2 □ 3 □ 4 □ 5 □ 10 □ More □
Trains?	1 □ 2 □ 3 □ 4 □ 5 □ 10 □ More □
Planes?	1 □ 2 □ 3 □ 4 □ 5 □ 10 □ More □
Who saw the first service station?	_________________________
Who saw the sea first?	_________________________
First asking to pee?	_________________________
First to say I'm hungry?	_________________________
First to say I'm thirsty?	_________________________
First to say *"Are we nearly there yet?"*	_________________________
Winner of dead lions?	_________________________

Who is in car?

____

____

____

Car colours:	Red ▢ Blue ▢ Green ▢ Yellow ▢
	Black ▢ White ▢ Silver ▢ Other ▢
Coaches?	1 ▢ 10 ▢ 20 ▢ 30 ▢ 40 ▢ 50 ▢ More ▢
Lorries?	1 ▢ 10 ▢ 20 ▢ 30 ▢ 40 ▢ 50 ▢ More ▢
Motor Bikes?	1 ▢ 10 ▢ 20 ▢ 30 ▢ 40 ▢ 50 ▢ More ▢
Caravans?	
Police Cars?	1 ▢ 2 ▢ 3 ▢ 4 ▢ 5 ▢ 10 ▢ More ▢
Cows?	1 ▢ 5 ▢ 10 ▢ 15 ▢ 20 ▢ 30 ▢ More ▢
Sheep?	1 ▢ 5 ▢ 10 ▢ 15 ▢ 20 ▢ 30 ▢ More ▢
Horses?	1 ▢ 5 ▢ 10 ▢ 15 ▢ 20 ▢ 30 ▢ More ▢
Windmills?	1 ▢ 2 ▢ 3 ▢ 4 ▢ 5 ▢ 10 ▢ More ▢
Trains?	1 ▢ 2 ▢ 3 ▢ 4 ▢ 5 ▢ 10 ▢ More ▢
Planes?	1 ▢ 2 ▢ 3 ▢ 4 ▢ 5 ▢ 10 ▢ More ▢
Who saw the first service station?	_________________________
Who saw the sea first?	_________________________
First asking to pee?	_________________________
First to say I'm hungry?	_________________________
First to say I'm thirsty?	_________________________
First to say *"Are we nearly there yet?"*	_________________________
Winner of dead lions?	_________________________

Who is in car?

____

____

____

Car colours:	Red ▢ Blue ▢ Green ▢ Yellow ▢
	Black ▢ White ▢ Silver ▢ Other ▢
Coaches?	1 ▢ 10 ▢ 20 ▢ 30 ▢ 40 ▢ 50 ▢ More ▢
Lorries?	1 ▢ 10 ▢ 20 ▢ 30 ▢ 40 ▢ 50 ▢ More ▢
Motor Bikes?	1 ▢ 10 ▢ 20 ▢ 30 ▢ 40 ▢ 50 ▢ More ▢
Caravans?	
Police Cars?	1 ▢ 2 ▢ 3 ▢ 4 ▢ 5 ▢ 10 ▢ More ▢
Cows?	1 ▢ 5 ▢ 10 ▢ 15 ▢ 20 ▢ 30 ▢ More ▢
Sheep?	1 ▢ 5 ▢ 10 ▢ 15 ▢ 20 ▢ 30 ▢ More ▢
Horses?	1 ▢ 5 ▢ 10 ▢ 15 ▢ 20 ▢ 30 ▢ More ▢
Windmills?	1 ▢ 2 ▢ 3 ▢ 4 ▢ 5 ▢ 10 ▢ More ▢
Trains?	1 ▢ 2 ▢ 3 ▢ 4 ▢ 5 ▢ 10 ▢ More ▢
Planes?	1 ▢ 2 ▢ 3 ▢ 4 ▢ 5 ▢ 10 ▢ More ▢

Who saw the first service station?   _______________________________

Who saw the sea first?   _______________________________

First asking to pee?   _______________________________

First to say I'm hungry?   _______________________________

First to say I'm thirsty?   _______________________________

First to say *"Are we nearly there yet?"*   _______________________________

Winner of dead lions?   _______________________________

Who is in car? _______________________
____
____

Car colours:	Red □ Blue □ Green □ Yellow □
	Black □ White □ Silver □ Other □
Coaches?	1 □ 10 □ 20 □ 30 □ 40 □ 50 □ More □
Lorries?	1 □ 10 □ 20 □ 30 □ 40 □ 50 □ More □
Motor Bikes?	1 □ 10 □ 20 □ 30 □ 40 □ 50 □ More □
Caravans?	
Police Cars?	1 □ 2 □ 3 □ 4 □ 5 □ 10 □ More □
Cows?	1 □ 5 □ 10 □ 15 □ 20 □ 30 □ More □
Sheep?	1 □ 5 □ 10 □ 15 □ 20 □ 30 □ More □
Horses?	1 □ 5 □ 10 □ 15 □ 20 □ 30 □ More □
Windmills?	1 □ 2 □ 3 □ 4 □ 5 □ 10 □ More □
Trains?	1 □ 2 □ 3 □ 4 □ 5 □ 10 □ More □
Planes?	1 □ 2 □ 3 □ 4 □ 5 □ 10 □ More □
Who saw the first service station?	_______________________
Who saw the sea first?	_______________________
First asking to pee?	_______________________
First to say I'm hungry?	_______________________
First to say I'm thirsty?	_______________________
First to say *"Are we nearly there yet?"*	_______________________
Winner of dead lions?	_______________________

Who is in car? ______________________________
____
____

Car colours:	Red ☐ Blue ☐ Green ☐ Yellow ☐
	Black ☐ White ☐ Silver ☐ Other ☐
Coaches?	1 ☐ 10 ☐ 20 ☐ 30 ☐ 40 ☐ 50 ☐ More ☐
Lorries?	1 ☐ 10 ☐ 20 ☐ 30 ☐ 40 ☐ 50 ☐ More ☐
Motor Bikes?	1 ☐ 10 ☐ 20 ☐ 30 ☐ 40 ☐ 50 ☐ More ☐
Caravans?	
Police Cars?	1 ☐ 2 ☐ 3 ☐ 4 ☐ 5 ☐ 10 ☐ More ☐
Cows?	1 ☐ 5 ☐ 10 ☐ 15 ☐ 20 ☐ 30 ☐ More ☐
Sheep?	1 ☐ 5 ☐ 10 ☐ 15 ☐ 20 ☐ 30 ☐ More ☐
Horses?	1 ☐ 5 ☐ 10 ☐ 15 ☐ 20 ☐ 30 ☐ More ☐
Windmills?	1 ☐ 2 ☐ 3 ☐ 4 ☐ 5 ☐ 10 ☐ More ☐
Trains?	1 ☐ 2 ☐ 3 ☐ 4 ☐ 5 ☐ 10 ☐ More ☐
Planes?	1 ☐ 2 ☐ 3 ☐ 4 ☐ 5 ☐ 10 ☐ More ☐
Who saw the first service station?	______________________________
Who saw the sea first?	______________________________
First asking to pee?	______________________________
First to say I'm hungry?	______________________________
First to say I'm thirsty?	______________________________
First to say *"Are we nearly there yet?"*	______________________________
Winner of dead lions?	______________________________

Who is in car?

____
____
____

Car colours:	Red □ Blue □ Green □ Yellow □ Black □ White □ Silver □ Other □
Coaches?	1 □ 10 □ 20 □ 30 □ 40 □ 50 □ More □
Lorries?	1 □ 10 □ 20 □ 30 □ 40 □ 50 □ More □
Motor Bikes?	1 □ 10 □ 20 □ 30 □ 40 □ 50 □ More □
Caravans?	
Police Cars?	1 □ 2 □ 3 □ 4 □ 5 □ 10 □ More □
Cows?	1 □ 5 □ 10 □ 15 □ 20 □ 30 □ More □
Sheep?	1 □ 5 □ 10 □ 15 □ 20 □ 30 □ More □
Horses?	1 □ 5 □ 10 □ 15 □ 20 □ 30 □ More □
Windmills?	1 □ 2 □ 3 □ 4 □ 5 □ 10 □ More □
Trains?	1 □ 2 □ 3 □ 4 □ 5 □ 10 □ More □
Planes?	1 □ 2 □ 3 □ 4 □ 5 □ 10 □ More □
Who saw the first service station?	_____________________
Who saw the sea first?	_____________________
First asking to pee?	_____________________
First to say I'm hungry?	_____________________
First to say I'm thirsty?	_____________________
First to say *"Are we nearly there yet?"*	_____________________
Winner of dead lions?	_____________________

Who is in car? ____________________
____
____

Car colours: Red □ Blue □ Green □ Yellow □

                            Black □ White □ Silver □ Other □

Coaches?   1 □ 10 □ 20 □ 30 □ 40 □ 50 □ More □

Lorries?   1 □ 10 □ 20 □ 30 □ 40 □ 50 □ More □

Motor Bikes?   1 □ 10 □ 20 □ 30 □ 40 □ 50 □ More □

Caravans?

Police Cars?   1 □ 2 □ 3 □ 4 □ 5 □ 10 □ More □

Cows?   1 □ 5 □ 10 □ 15 □ 20 □ 30 □ More □

Sheep?   1 □ 5 □ 10 □ 15 □ 20 □ 30 □ More □

Horses?   1 □ 5 □ 10 □ 15 □ 20 □ 30 □ More □

Windmills?   1 □ 2 □ 3 □ 4 □ 5 □ 10 □ More □

Trains?   1 □ 2 □ 3 □ 4 □ 5 □ 10 □ More □

Planes?   1 □ 2 □ 3 □ 4 □ 5 □ 10 □ More □

Who saw the first service
station?   ____________________

Who saw the sea first?   ____________________

First asking to pee?   ____________________

First to say I'm hungry?   ____________________

First to say I'm thirsty?   ____________________

First to say *"Are we nearly
there yet?"*   ____________________

Winner of dead lions?   ____________________

Who is in car?

____

____

____

Car colours:	Red □ Blue □ Green □ Yellow □ Black □ White □ Silver □ Other □
Coaches?	1 □ 10 □ 20 □ 30 □ 40 □ 50 □ More □
Lorries?	1 □ 10 □ 20 □ 30 □ 40 □ 50 □ More □
Motor Bikes?	1 □ 10 □ 20 □ 30 □ 40 □ 50 □ More □
Caravans?	
Police Cars?	1 □ 2 □ 3 □ 4 □ 5 □ 10 □ More □
Cows?	1 □ 5 □ 10 □ 15 □ 20 □ 30 □ More □
Sheep?	1 □ 5 □ 10 □ 15 □ 20 □ 30 □ More □
Horses?	1 □ 5 □ 10 □ 15 □ 20 □ 30 □ More □
Windmills?	1 □ 2 □ 3 □ 4 □ 5 □ 10 □ More □
Trains?	1 □ 2 □ 3 □ 4 □ 5 □ 10 □ More □
Planes?	1 □ 2 □ 3 □ 4 □ 5 □ 10 □ More □
Who saw the first service station?	_________________________
Who saw the sea first?	_________________________
First asking to pee?	_________________________
First to say I'm hungry?	_________________________
First to say I'm thirsty?	_________________________
First to say *"Are we nearly there yet?"*	_________________________
Winner of dead lions?	_________________________

Who is in car?

____

____

____

Car colours:	Red □ Blue □ Green □ Yellow □
	Black □ White □ Silver □ Other □
Coaches?	1 □ 10 □ 20 □ 30 □ 40 □ 50 □ More □
Lorries?	1 □ 10 □ 20 □ 30 □ 40 □ 50 □ More □
Motor Bikes?	1 □ 10 □ 20 □ 30 □ 40 □ 50 □ More □
Caravans?	
Police Cars?	1 □ 2 □ 3 □ 4 □ 5 □ 10 □ More □
Cows?	1 □ 5 □ 10 □ 15 □ 20 □ 30 □ More □
Sheep?	1 □ 5 □ 10 □ 15 □ 20 □ 30 □ More □
Horses?	1 □ 5 □ 10 □ 15 □ 20 □ 30 □ More □
Windmills?	1 □ 2 □ 3 □ 4 □ 5 □ 10 □ More □
Trains?	1 □ 2 □ 3 □ 4 □ 5 □ 10 □ More □
Planes?	1 □ 2 □ 3 □ 4 □ 5 □ 10 □ More □
Who saw the first service station?	_____________________
Who saw the sea first?	_____________________
First asking to pee?	_____________________
First to say I'm hungry?	_____________________
First to say I'm thirsty?	_____________________
First to say *"Are we nearly there yet?"*	_____________________
Winner of dead lions?	_____________________

Who is in car?

____

____

____

Car colours:	Red □ Blue □ Green □ Yellow □
	Black □ White □ Silver □ Other □
Coaches?	1 □ 10 □ 20 □ 30 □ 40 □ 50 □ More □
Lorries?	1 □ 10 □ 20 □ 30 □ 40 □ 50 □ More □
Motor Bikes?	1 □ 10 □ 20 □ 30 □ 40 □ 50 □ More □
Caravans?	
Police Cars?	1 □ 2 □ 3 □ 4 □ 5 □ 10 □ More □
Cows?	1 □ 5 □ 10 □ 15 □ 20 □ 30 □ More □
Sheep?	1 □ 5 □ 10 □ 15 □ 20 □ 30 □ More □
Horses?	1 □ 5 □ 10 □ 15 □ 20 □ 30 □ More □
Windmills?	1 □ 2 □ 3 □ 4 □ 5 □ 10 □ More □
Trains?	1 □ 2 □ 3 □ 4 □ 5 □ 10 □ More □
Planes?	1 □ 2 □ 3 □ 4 □ 5 □ 10 □ More □
Who saw the first service station?	_____________________
Who saw the sea first?	_____________________
First asking to pee?	_____________________
First to say I'm hungry?	_____________________
First to say I'm thirsty?	_____________________
First to say *"Are we nearly there yet?"*	_____________________
Winner of dead lions?	_____________________

Who is in car? ______________________________
____
____

Car colours:	Red ☐ Blue ☐ Green ☐ Yellow ☐
	Black ☐ White ☐ Silver ☐ Other ☐
Coaches?	1 ☐ 10 ☐ 20 ☐ 30 ☐ 40 ☐ 50 ☐ More ☐
Lorries?	1 ☐ 10 ☐ 20 ☐ 30 ☐ 40 ☐ 50 ☐ More ☐
Motor Bikes?	1 ☐ 10 ☐ 20 ☐ 30 ☐ 40 ☐ 50 ☐ More ☐
Caravans?	
Police Cars?	1 ☐ 2 ☐ 3 ☐ 4 ☐ 5 ☐ 10 ☐ More ☐
Cows?	1 ☐ 5 ☐ 10 ☐ 15 ☐ 20 ☐ 30 ☐ More ☐
Sheep?	1 ☐ 5 ☐ 10 ☐ 15 ☐ 20 ☐ 30 ☐ More ☐
Horses?	1 ☐ 5 ☐ 10 ☐ 15 ☐ 20 ☐ 30 ☐ More ☐
Windmills?	1 ☐ 2 ☐ 3 ☐ 4 ☐ 5 ☐ 10 ☐ More ☐
Trains?	1 ☐ 2 ☐ 3 ☐ 4 ☐ 5 ☐ 10 ☐ More ☐
Planes?	1 ☐ 2 ☐ 3 ☐ 4 ☐ 5 ☐ 10 ☐ More ☐
Who saw the first service station?	______________________________
Who saw the sea first?	______________________________
First asking to pee?	______________________________
First to say I'm hungry?	______________________________
First to say I'm thirsty?	______________________________
First to say *"Are we nearly there yet?"*	______________________________
Winner of dead lions?	______________________________

Who is in car?

____

____

____

Car colours: Red □ Blue □ Green □ Yellow □

Black □ White □ Silver □ Other □

Coaches?   1 □ 10 □ 20 □ 30 □ 40 □ 50 □ More □

Lorries?   1 □ 10 □ 20 □ 30 □ 40 □ 50 □ More □

Motor Bikes?   1 □ 10 □ 20 □ 30 □ 40 □ 50 □ More □

Caravans?

Police Cars?   1 □ 2 □ 3 □ 4 □ 5 □ 10 □ More □

Cows?   1 □ 5 □ 10 □ 15 □ 20 □ 30 □ More □

Sheep?   1 □ 5 □ 10 □ 15 □ 20 □ 30 □ More □

Horses?   1 □ 5 □ 10 □ 15 □ 20 □ 30 □ More □

Windmills?   1 □ 2 □ 3 □ 4 □ 5 □ 10 □ More □

Trains?   1 □ 2 □ 3 □ 4 □ 5 □ 10 □ More □

Planes?   1 □ 2 □ 3 □ 4 □ 5 □ 10 □ More □

Who saw the first service station?   ___________________________

Who saw the sea first?   ___________________________

First asking to pee?   ___________________________

First to say I'm hungry?   ___________________________

First to say I'm thirsty?   ___________________________

First to say *"Are we nearly there yet?"*   ___________________________

Winner of dead lions?   ___________________________

Who is in car?

____

____

____

Car colours:	Red □ Blue □ Green □ Yellow □
	Black □ White □ Silver □ Other □
Coaches?	1 □ 10 □ 20 □ 30 □ 40 □ 50 □ More □
Lorries?	1 □ 10 □ 20 □ 30 □ 40 □ 50 □ More □
Motor Bikes?	1 □ 10 □ 20 □ 30 □ 40 □ 50 □ More □
Caravans?	
Police Cars?	1 □ 2 □ 3 □ 4 □ 5 □ 10 □ More □
Cows?	1 □ 5 □ 10 □ 15 □ 20 □ 30 □ More □
Sheep?	1 □ 5 □ 10 □ 15 □ 20 □ 30 □ More □
Horses?	1 □ 5 □ 10 □ 15 □ 20 □ 30 □ More □
Windmills?	1 □ 2 □ 3 □ 4 □ 5 □ 10 □ More □
Trains?	1 □ 2 □ 3 □ 4 □ 5 □ 10 □ More □
Planes?	1 □ 2 □ 3 □ 4 □ 5 □ 10 □ More □
Who saw the first service station?	_______________________
Who saw the sea first?	_______________________
First asking to pee?	_______________________
First to say I'm hungry?	_______________________
First to say I'm thirsty?	_______________________
First to say *"Are we nearly there yet?"*	_______________________
Winner of dead lions?	_______________________

Who is in car?

____

____

____

Car colours:	Red □ Blue □ Green □ Yellow □
	Black □ White □ Silver □ Other □
Coaches?	1 □ 10 □ 20 □ 30 □ 40 □ 50 □ More □
Lorries?	1 □ 10 □ 20 □ 30 □ 40 □ 50 □ More □
Motor Bikes?	1 □ 10 □ 20 □ 30 □ 40 □ 50 □ More □
Caravans?	
Police Cars?	1 □ 2 □ 3 □ 4 □ 5 □ 10 □ More □
Cows?	1 □ 5 □ 10 □ 15 □ 20 □ 30 □ More □
Sheep?	1 □ 5 □ 10 □ 15 □ 20 □ 30 □ More □
Horses?	1 □ 5 □ 10 □ 15 □ 20 □ 30 □ More □
Windmills?	1 □ 2 □ 3 □ 4 □ 5 □ 10 □ More □
Trains?	1 □ 2 □ 3 □ 4 □ 5 □ 10 □ More □
Planes?	1 □ 2 □ 3 □ 4 □ 5 □ 10 □ More □
Who saw the first service station?	____________________
Who saw the sea first?	____________________
First asking to pee?	____________________
First to say I'm hungry?	____________________
First to say I'm thirsty?	____________________
First to say *"Are we nearly there yet?"*	____________________
Winner of dead lions?	____________________

Who is in car?

____

____

____

Car colours:	Red ☐ Blue ☐ Green ☐ Yellow ☐
	Black ☐ White ☐ Silver ☐ Other ☐
Coaches?	1 ☐ 10 ☐ 20 ☐ 30 ☐ 40 ☐ 50 ☐ More ☐
Lorries?	1 ☐ 10 ☐ 20 ☐ 30 ☐ 40 ☐ 50 ☐ More ☐
Motor Bikes?	1 ☐ 10 ☐ 20 ☐ 30 ☐ 40 ☐ 50 ☐ More ☐
Caravans?	
Police Cars?	1 ☐ 2 ☐ 3 ☐ 4 ☐ 5 ☐ 10 ☐ More ☐
Cows?	1 ☐ 5 ☐ 10 ☐ 15 ☐ 20 ☐ 30 ☐ More ☐
Sheep?	1 ☐ 5 ☐ 10 ☐ 15 ☐ 20 ☐ 30 ☐ More ☐
Horses?	1 ☐ 5 ☐ 10 ☐ 15 ☐ 20 ☐ 30 ☐ More ☐
Windmills?	1 ☐ 2 ☐ 3 ☐ 4 ☐ 5 ☐ 10 ☐ More ☐
Trains?	1 ☐ 2 ☐ 3 ☐ 4 ☐ 5 ☐ 10 ☐ More ☐
Planes?	1 ☐ 2 ☐ 3 ☐ 4 ☐ 5 ☐ 10 ☐ More ☐
Who saw the first service station?	_______________________
Who saw the sea first?	_______________________
First asking to pee?	_______________________
First to say I'm hungry?	_______________________
First to say I'm thirsty?	_______________________
First to say *"Are we nearly there yet?"*	_______________________
Winner of dead lions?	_______________________

<table>
<tr><td>

Who is in car?

</td><td>

____
____
____

</td></tr>
</table>

Car colours:	Red ☐ Blue ☐ Green ☐ Yellow ☐
	Black ☐ White ☐ Silver ☐ Other ☐
Coaches?	1 ☐ 10 ☐ 20 ☐ 30 ☐ 40 ☐ 50 ☐ More ☐
Lorries?	1 ☐ 10 ☐ 20 ☐ 30 ☐ 40 ☐ 50 ☐ More ☐
Motor Bikes?	1 ☐ 10 ☐ 20 ☐ 30 ☐ 40 ☐ 50 ☐ More ☐
Caravans?	
Police Cars?	1 ☐ 2 ☐ 3 ☐ 4 ☐ 5 ☐ 10 ☐ More ☐
Cows?	1 ☐ 5 ☐ 10 ☐ 15 ☐ 20 ☐ 30 ☐ More ☐
Sheep?	1 ☐ 5 ☐ 10 ☐ 15 ☐ 20 ☐ 30 ☐ More ☐
Horses?	1 ☐ 5 ☐ 10 ☐ 15 ☐ 20 ☐ 30 ☐ More ☐
Windmills?	1 ☐ 2 ☐ 3 ☐ 4 ☐ 5 ☐ 10 ☐ More ☐
Trains?	1 ☐ 2 ☐ 3 ☐ 4 ☐ 5 ☐ 10 ☐ More ☐
Planes?	1 ☐ 2 ☐ 3 ☐ 4 ☐ 5 ☐ 10 ☐ More ☐
Who saw the first service station?	_______________________
Who saw the sea first?	_______________________
First asking to pee?	_______________________
First to say I'm hungry?	_______________________
First to say I'm thirsty?	_______________________
First to say *"Are we nearly there yet?"*	_______________________
Winner of dead lions?	_______________________

Who is in car? ______________________________
____
____

Car colours:	Red □ Blue □ Green □ Yellow □
	Black □ White □ Silver □ Other □
Coaches?	1 □ 10 □ 20 □ 30 □ 40 □ 50 □ More □
Lorries?	1 □ 10 □ 20 □ 30 □ 40 □ 50 □ More □
Motor Bikes?	1 □ 10 □ 20 □ 30 □ 40 □ 50 □ More □
Caravans?	
Police Cars?	1 □ 2 □ 3 □ 4 □ 5 □ 10 □ More □
Cows?	1 □ 5 □ 10 □ 15 □ 20 □ 30 □ More □
Sheep?	1 □ 5 □ 10 □ 15 □ 20 □ 30 □ More □
Horses?	1 □ 5 □ 10 □ 15 □ 20 □ 30 □ More □
Windmills?	1 □ 2 □ 3 □ 4 □ 5 □ 10 □ More □
Trains?	1 □ 2 □ 3 □ 4 □ 5 □ 10 □ More □
Planes?	1 □ 2 □ 3 □ 4 □ 5 □ 10 □ More □
Who saw the first service station?	____________________
Who saw the sea first?	____________________
First asking to pee?	____________________
First to say I'm hungry?	____________________
First to say I'm thirsty?	____________________
First to say *"Are we nearly there yet?"*	____________________
Winner of dead lions?	____________________

Who is in car?

____

____

____

Car colours:	Red □ Blue □ Green □ Yellow □
	Black □ White □ Silver □ Other □
Coaches?	1 □ 10 □ 20 □ 30 □ 40 □ 50 □ More □
Lorries?	1 □ 10 □ 20 □ 30 □ 40 □ 50 □ More □
Motor Bikes?	1 □ 10 □ 20 □ 30 □ 40 □ 50 □ More □
Caravans?	
Police Cars?	1 □ 2 □ 3 □ 4 □ 5 □ 10 □ More □
Cows?	1 □ 5 □ 10 □ 15 □ 20 □ 30 □ More □
Sheep?	1 □ 5 □ 10 □ 15 □ 20 □ 30 □ More □
Horses?	1 □ 5 □ 10 □ 15 □ 20 □ 30 □ More □
Windmills?	1 □ 2 □ 3 □ 4 □ 5 □ 10 □ More □
Trains?	1 □ 2 □ 3 □ 4 □ 5 □ 10 □ More □
Planes?	1 □ 2 □ 3 □ 4 □ 5 □ 10 □ More □

Who saw the first service station?   ____________________

Who saw the sea first?   ____________________

First asking to pee?   ____________________

First to say I'm hungry?   ____________________

First to say I'm thirsty?   ____________________

First to say *"Are we nearly there yet?"*   ____________________

Winner of dead lions?   ____________________

Who is in car?

____

____

____

Car colours:	Red □ Blue □ Green □ Yellow □ Black □ White □ Silver □ Other □
Coaches?	1 □ 10 □ 20 □ 30 □ 40 □ 50 □ More □
Lorries?	1 □ 10 □ 20 □ 30 □ 40 □ 50 □ More □
Motor Bikes?	1 □ 10 □ 20 □ 30 □ 40 □ 50 □ More □
Caravans?	
Police Cars?	1 □ 2 □ 3 □ 4 □ 5 □ 10 □ More □
Cows?	1 □ 5 □ 10 □ 15 □ 20 □ 30 □ More □
Sheep?	1 □ 5 □ 10 □ 15 □ 20 □ 30 □ More □
Horses?	1 □ 5 □ 10 □ 15 □ 20 □ 30 □ More □
Windmills?	1 □ 2 □ 3 □ 4 □ 5 □ 10 □ More □
Trains?	1 □ 2 □ 3 □ 4 □ 5 □ 10 □ More □
Planes?	1 □ 2 □ 3 □ 4 □ 5 □ 10 □ More □
Who saw the first service station?	__________________________
Who saw the sea first?	__________________________
First asking to pee?	__________________________
First to say I'm hungry?	__________________________
First to say I'm thirsty?	__________________________
First to say *"Are we nearly there yet?"*	__________________________
Winner of dead lions?	__________________________

Who is in car?

____
____
____

Car colours:	Red □ Blue □ Green □ Yellow □
	Black □ White □ Silver □ Other □
Coaches?	1 □ 10 □ 20 □ 30 □ 40 □ 50 □ More □
Lorries?	1 □ 10 □ 20 □ 30 □ 40 □ 50 □ More □
Motor Bikes?	1 □ 10 □ 20 □ 30 □ 40 □ 50 □ More □
Caravans?	
Police Cars?	1 □ 2 □ 3 □ 4 □ 5 □ 10 □ More □
Cows?	1 □ 5 □ 10 □ 15 □ 20 □ 30 □ More □
Sheep?	1 □ 5 □ 10 □ 15 □ 20 □ 30 □ More □
Horses?	1 □ 5 □ 10 □ 15 □ 20 □ 30 □ More □
Windmills?	1 □ 2 □ 3 □ 4 □ 5 □ 10 □ More □
Trains?	1 □ 2 □ 3 □ 4 □ 5 □ 10 □ More □
Planes?	1 □ 2 □ 3 □ 4 □ 5 □ 10 □ More □

Who saw the first service station? _______________________________

Who saw the sea first? _______________________________

First asking to pee? _______________________________

First to say I'm hungry? _______________________________

First to say I'm thirsty? _______________________________

First to say *"Are we nearly there yet?"* _______________________________

Winner of dead lions? _______________________________

Car colours:	Red □ Blue □ Green □ Yellow □
	Black □ White □ Silver □ Other □
Coaches?	1 □ 10 □ 20 □ 30 □ 40 □ 50 □ More □
Lorries?	1 □ 10 □ 20 □ 30 □ 40 □ 50 □ More □
Motor Bikes?	1 □ 10 □ 20 □ 30 □ 40 □ 50 □ More □
Caravans?	
Police Cars?	1 □ 2 □ 3 □ 4 □ 5 □ 10 □ More □
Cows?	1 □ 5 □ 10 □ 15 □ 20 □ 30 □ More □
Sheep?	1 □ 5 □ 10 □ 15 □ 20 □ 30 □ More □
Horses?	1 □ 5 □ 10 □ 15 □ 20 □ 30 □ More □
Windmills?	1 □ 2 □ 3 □ 4 □ 5 □ 10 □ More □
Trains?	1 □ 2 □ 3 □ 4 □ 5 □ 10 □ More □
Planes?	1 □ 2 □ 3 □ 4 □ 5 □ 10 □ More □
Who saw the first service station?	________________
Who saw the sea first?	________________
First asking to pee?	________________
First to say I'm hungry?	________________
First to say I'm thirsty?	________________
First to say *"Are we nearly there yet?"*	________________
Winner of dead lions?	________________

Who is in car?

____

____

____

Car colours:	Red □ Blue □ Green □ Yellow □
	Black □ White □ Silver □ Other □
Coaches?	1 □ 10 □ 20 □ 30 □ 40 □ 50 □ More □
Lorries?	1 □ 10 □ 20 □ 30 □ 40 □ 50 □ More □
Motor Bikes?	1 □ 10 □ 20 □ 30 □ 40 □ 50 □ More □
Caravans?	
Police Cars?	1 □ 2 □ 3 □ 4 □ 5 □ 10 □ More □
Cows?	1 □ 5 □ 10 □ 15 □ 20 □ 30 □ More □
Sheep?	1 □ 5 □ 10 □ 15 □ 20 □ 30 □ More □
Horses?	1 □ 5 □ 10 □ 15 □ 20 □ 30 □ More □
Windmills?	1 □ 2 □ 3 □ 4 □ 5 □ 10 □ More □
Trains?	1 □ 2 □ 3 □ 4 □ 5 □ 10 □ More □
Planes?	1 □ 2 □ 3 □ 4 □ 5 □ 10 □ More □
Who saw the first service station?	______________________
Who saw the sea first?	______________________
First asking to pee?	______________________
First to say I'm hungry?	______________________
First to say I'm thirsty?	______________________
First to say *"Are we nearly there yet?"*	______________________
Winner of dead lions?	______________________

Who is in car? ______________________________
____
____

Car colours:	Red □ Blue □ Green □ Yellow □
	Black □ White □ Silver □ Other □
Coaches?	1 □ 10 □ 20 □ 30 □ 40 □ 50 □ More □
Lorries?	1 □ 10 □ 20 □ 30 □ 40 □ 50 □ More □
Motor Bikes?	1 □ 10 □ 20 □ 30 □ 40 □ 50 □ More □
Caravans?	
Police Cars?	1 □ 2 □ 3 □ 4 □ 5 □ 10 □ More □
Cows?	1 □ 5 □ 10 □ 15 □ 20 □ 30 □ More □
Sheep?	1 □ 5 □ 10 □ 15 □ 20 □ 30 □ More □
Horses?	1 □ 5 □ 10 □ 15 □ 20 □ 30 □ More □
Windmills?	1 □ 2 □ 3 □ 4 □ 5 □ 10 □ More □
Trains?	1 □ 2 □ 3 □ 4 □ 5 □ 10 □ More □
Planes?	1 □ 2 □ 3 □ 4 □ 5 □ 10 □ More □
Who saw the first service station?	_______________________
Who saw the sea first?	_______________________
First asking to pee?	_______________________
First to say I'm hungry?	_______________________
First to say I'm thirsty?	_______________________
First to say *"Are we nearly there yet?"*	_______________________
Winner of dead lions?	_______________________

Who is in car?

____

____

____

Car colours:	Red □ Blue □ Green □ Yellow □
	Black □ White □ Silver □ Other □
Coaches?	1 □ 10 □ 20 □ 30 □ 40 □ 50 □ More □
Lorries?	1 □ 10 □ 20 □ 30 □ 40 □ 50 □ More □
Motor Bikes?	1 □ 10 □ 20 □ 30 □ 40 □ 50 □ More □
Caravans?	
Police Cars?	1 □ 2 □ 3 □ 4 □ 5 □ 10 □ More □
Cows?	1 □ 5 □ 10 □ 15 □ 20 □ 30 □ More □
Sheep?	1 □ 5 □ 10 □ 15 □ 20 □ 30 □ More □
Horses?	1 □ 5 □ 10 □ 15 □ 20 □ 30 □ More □
Windmills?	1 □ 2 □ 3 □ 4 □ 5 □ 10 □ More □
Trains?	1 □ 2 □ 3 □ 4 □ 5 □ 10 □ More □
Planes?	1 □ 2 □ 3 □ 4 □ 5 □ 10 □ More □
Who saw the first service station?	_______________________
Who saw the sea first?	_______________________
First asking to pee?	_______________________
First to say I'm hungry?	_______________________
First to say I'm thirsty?	_______________________
First to say *"Are we nearly there yet?"*	_______________________
Winner of dead lions?	_______________________

Who is in car? ______________________
____
____

Car colours:	Red □ Blue □ Green □ Yellow □ Black □ White □ Silver □ Other □
Coaches?	1 □ 10 □ 20 □ 30 □ 40 □ 50 □ More □
Lorries?	1 □ 10 □ 20 □ 30 □ 40 □ 50 □ More □
Motor Bikes?	1 □ 10 □ 20 □ 30 □ 40 □ 50 □ More □
Caravans?	
Police Cars?	1 □ 2 □ 3 □ 4 □ 5 □ 10 □ More □
Cows?	1 □ 5 □ 10 □ 15 □ 20 □ 30 □ More □
Sheep?	1 □ 5 □ 10 □ 15 □ 20 □ 30 □ More □
Horses?	1 □ 5 □ 10 □ 15 □ 20 □ 30 □ More □
Windmills?	1 □ 2 □ 3 □ 4 □ 5 □ 10 □ More □
Trains?	1 □ 2 □ 3 □ 4 □ 5 □ 10 □ More □
Planes?	1 □ 2 □ 3 □ 4 □ 5 □ 10 □ More □
Who saw the first service station?	____________________
Who saw the sea first?	____________________
First asking to pee?	____________________
First to say I'm hungry?	____________________
First to say I'm thirsty?	____________________
First to say *"Are we nearly there yet?"*	____________________
Winner of dead lions?	____________________

Who is in car? ______________________

____

____

Car colours:	Red ☐ Blue ☐ Green ☐ Yellow ☐
	Black ☐ White ☐ Silver ☐ Other ☐
Coaches?	1 ☐ 10 ☐ 20 ☐ 30 ☐ 40 ☐ 50 ☐ More ☐
Lorries?	1 ☐ 10 ☐ 20 ☐ 30 ☐ 40 ☐ 50 ☐ More ☐
Motor Bikes?	1 ☐ 10 ☐ 20 ☐ 30 ☐ 40 ☐ 50 ☐ More ☐
Caravans?	
Police Cars?	1 ☐ 2 ☐ 3 ☐ 4 ☐ 5 ☐ 10 ☐ More ☐
Cows?	1 ☐ 5 ☐ 10 ☐ 15 ☐ 20 ☐ 30 ☐ More ☐
Sheep?	1 ☐ 5 ☐ 10 ☐ 15 ☐ 20 ☐ 30 ☐ More ☐
Horses?	1 ☐ 5 ☐ 10 ☐ 15 ☐ 20 ☐ 30 ☐ More ☐
Windmills?	1 ☐ 2 ☐ 3 ☐ 4 ☐ 5 ☐ 10 ☐ More ☐
Trains?	1 ☐ 2 ☐ 3 ☐ 4 ☐ 5 ☐ 10 ☐ More ☐
Planes?	1 ☐ 2 ☐ 3 ☐ 4 ☐ 5 ☐ 10 ☐ More ☐
Who saw the first service station?	______________________
Who saw the sea first?	______________________
First asking to pee?	______________________
First to say I'm hungry?	______________________
First to say I'm thirsty?	______________________
First to say *"Are we nearly there yet?"*	______________________
Winner of dead lions?	______________________

Who is in car?

____

____

____

Car colours: Red ☐ Blue ☐ Green ☐ Yellow ☐

Black ☐ White ☐ Silver ☐ Other ☐

Coaches? 1 ☐ 10 ☐ 20 ☐ 30 ☐ 40 ☐ 50 ☐ More ☐

Lorries? 1 ☐ 10 ☐ 20 ☐ 30 ☐ 40 ☐ 50 ☐ More ☐

Motor Bikes? 1 ☐ 10 ☐ 20 ☐ 30 ☐ 40 ☐ 50 ☐ More ☐

Caravans?

Police Cars? 1 ☐ 2 ☐ 3 ☐ 4 ☐ 5 ☐ 10 ☐ More ☐

Cows? 1 ☐ 5 ☐ 10 ☐ 15 ☐ 20 ☐ 30 ☐ More ☐

Sheep? 1 ☐ 5 ☐ 10 ☐ 15 ☐ 20 ☐ 30 ☐ More ☐

Horses? 1 ☐ 5 ☐ 10 ☐ 15 ☐ 20 ☐ 30 ☐ More ☐

Windmills? 1 ☐ 2 ☐ 3 ☐ 4 ☐ 5 ☐ 10 ☐ More ☐

Trains? 1 ☐ 2 ☐ 3 ☐ 4 ☐ 5 ☐ 10 ☐ More ☐

Planes? 1 ☐ 2 ☐ 3 ☐ 4 ☐ 5 ☐ 10 ☐ More ☐

Who saw the first service station? _______________________

Who saw the sea first? _______________________

First asking to pee? _______________________

First to say I'm hungry? _______________________

First to say I'm thirsty? _______________________

First to say *"Are we nearly there yet?"* _______________________

Winner of dead lions? _______________________

Who is in car?

____

____

____

Car colours:	Red □ Blue □ Green □ Yellow □
	Black □ White □ Silver □ Other □
Coaches?	1 □ 10 □ 20 □ 30 □ 40 □ 50 □ More □
Lorries?	1 □ 10 □ 20 □ 30 □ 40 □ 50 □ More □
Motor Bikes?	1 □ 10 □ 20 □ 30 □ 40 □ 50 □ More □
Caravans?	
Police Cars?	1 □ 2 □ 3 □ 4 □ 5 □ 10 □ More □
Cows?	1 □ 5 □ 10 □ 15 □ 20 □ 30 □ More □
Sheep?	1 □ 5 □ 10 □ 15 □ 20 □ 30 □ More □
Horses?	1 □ 5 □ 10 □ 15 □ 20 □ 30 □ More □
Windmills?	1 □ 2 □ 3 □ 4 □ 5 □ 10 □ More □
Trains?	1 □ 2 □ 3 □ 4 □ 5 □ 10 □ More □
Planes?	1 □ 2 □ 3 □ 4 □ 5 □ 10 □ More □
Who saw the first service station?	__________________________
Who saw the sea first?	__________________________
First asking to pee?	__________________________
First to say I'm hungry?	__________________________
First to say I'm thirsty?	__________________________
First to say *"Are we nearly there yet?"*	__________________________
Winner of dead lions?	__________________________

Who is in car?

____
____
____

Car colours:	Red □ Blue □ Green □ Yellow □ Black □ White □ Silver □ Other □
Coaches?	1 □ 10 □ 20 □ 30 □ 40 □ 50 □ More □
Lorries?	1 □ 10 □ 20 □ 30 □ 40 □ 50 □ More □
Motor Bikes?	1 □ 10 □ 20 □ 30 □ 40 □ 50 □ More □
Caravans?	
Police Cars?	1 □ 2 □ 3 □ 4 □ 5 □ 10 □ More □
Cows?	1 □ 5 □ 10 □ 15 □ 20 □ 30 □ More □
Sheep?	1 □ 5 □ 10 □ 15 □ 20 □ 30 □ More □
Horses?	1 □ 5 □ 10 □ 15 □ 20 □ 30 □ More □
Windmills?	1 □ 2 □ 3 □ 4 □ 5 □ 10 □ More □
Trains?	1 □ 2 □ 3 □ 4 □ 5 □ 10 □ More □
Planes?	1 □ 2 □ 3 □ 4 □ 5 □ 10 □ More □

Who saw the first service station? ____________________________

Who saw the sea first? ____________________________

First asking to pee? ____________________________

First to say I'm hungry? ____________________________

First to say I'm thirsty? ____________________________

First to say *"Are we nearly there yet?"* ____________________________

Winner of dead lions? ____________________________

Who is in car?

____

____

____

Car colours:	Red □ Blue □ Green □ Yellow □
	Black □ White □ Silver □ Other □
Coaches?	1 □ 10 □ 20 □ 30 □ 40 □ 50 □ More □
Lorries?	1 □ 10 □ 20 □ 30 □ 40 □ 50 □ More □
Motor Bikes?	1 □ 10 □ 20 □ 30 □ 40 □ 50 □ More □
Caravans?	
Police Cars?	1 □ 2 □ 3 □ 4 □ 5 □ 10 □ More □
Cows?	1 □ 5 □ 10 □ 15 □ 20 □ 30 □ More □
Sheep?	1 □ 5 □ 10 □ 15 □ 20 □ 30 □ More □
Horses?	1 □ 5 □ 10 □ 15 □ 20 □ 30 □ More □
Windmills?	1 □ 2 □ 3 □ 4 □ 5 □ 10 □ More □
Trains?	1 □ 2 □ 3 □ 4 □ 5 □ 10 □ More □
Planes?	1 □ 2 □ 3 □ 4 □ 5 □ 10 □ More □

Who saw the first service station? _______________________________

Who saw the sea first? _______________________________

First asking to pee? _______________________________

First to say I'm hungry? _______________________________

First to say I'm thirsty? _______________________________

First to say *"Are we nearly there yet?"* _______________________________

Winner of dead lions? _______________________________

Who is in car?

____

____

____

Car colours:	Red □ Blue □ Green □ Yellow □
	Black □ White □ Silver □ Other □
Coaches?	1 □ 10 □ 20 □ 30 □ 40 □ 50 □ More □
Lorries?	1 □ 10 □ 20 □ 30 □ 40 □ 50 □ More □
Motor Bikes?	1 □ 10 □ 20 □ 30 □ 40 □ 50 □ More □
Caravans?	
Police Cars?	1 □ 2 □ 3 □ 4 □ 5 □ 10 □ More □
Cows?	1 □ 5 □ 10 □ 15 □ 20 □ 30 □ More □
Sheep?	1 □ 5 □ 10 □ 15 □ 20 □ 30 □ More □
Horses?	1 □ 5 □ 10 □ 15 □ 20 □ 30 □ More □
Windmills?	1 □ 2 □ 3 □ 4 □ 5 □ 10 □ More □
Trains?	1 □ 2 □ 3 □ 4 □ 5 □ 10 □ More □
Planes?	1 □ 2 □ 3 □ 4 □ 5 □ 10 □ More □
Who saw the first service station?	_______________________
Who saw the sea first?	_______________________
First asking to pee?	_______________________
First to say I'm hungry?	_______________________
First to say I'm thirsty?	_______________________
First to say *"Are we nearly there yet?"*	_______________________
Winner of dead lions?	_______________________

Who is in car?

____

____

____

Car colours:	Red ☐ Blue ☐ Green ☐ Yellow ☐
	Black ☐ White ☐ Silver ☐ Other ☐
Coaches?	1 ☐ 10 ☐ 20 ☐ 30 ☐ 40 ☐ 50 ☐ More ☐
Lorries?	1 ☐ 10 ☐ 20 ☐ 30 ☐ 40 ☐ 50 ☐ More ☐
Motor Bikes?	1 ☐ 10 ☐ 20 ☐ 30 ☐ 40 ☐ 50 ☐ More ☐
Caravans?	
Police Cars?	1 ☐ 2 ☐ 3 ☐ 4 ☐ 5 ☐ 10 ☐ More ☐
Cows?	1 ☐ 5 ☐ 10 ☐ 15 ☐ 20 ☐ 30 ☐ More ☐
Sheep?	1 ☐ 5 ☐ 10 ☐ 15 ☐ 20 ☐ 30 ☐ More ☐
Horses?	1 ☐ 5 ☐ 10 ☐ 15 ☐ 20 ☐ 30 ☐ More ☐
Windmills?	1 ☐ 2 ☐ 3 ☐ 4 ☐ 5 ☐ 10 ☐ More ☐
Trains?	1 ☐ 2 ☐ 3 ☐ 4 ☐ 5 ☐ 10 ☐ More ☐
Planes?	1 ☐ 2 ☐ 3 ☐ 4 ☐ 5 ☐ 10 ☐ More ☐

Who saw the first service station? _______________________

Who saw the sea first? _______________________

First asking to pee? _______________________

First to say I'm hungry? _______________________

First to say I'm thirsty? _______________________

First to say _"Are we nearly there yet?"_ _______________________

Winner of dead lions? _______________________

Who is in car?

____

____

____

Car colours: Red □ Blue □ Green □ Yellow □

Black □ White □ Silver □ Other □

Coaches?	1 □ 10 □ 20 □ 30 □ 40 □ 50 □ More □
Lorries?	1 □ 10 □ 20 □ 30 □ 40 □ 50 □ More □
Motor Bikes?	1 □ 10 □ 20 □ 30 □ 40 □ 50 □ More □
Caravans?	
Police Cars?	1 □ 2 □ 3 □ 4 □ 5 □ 10 □ More □
Cows?	1 □ 5 □ 10 □ 15 □ 20 □ 30 □ More □
Sheep?	1 □ 5 □ 10 □ 15 □ 20 □ 30 □ More □
Horses?	1 □ 5 □ 10 □ 15 □ 20 □ 30 □ More □
Windmills?	1 □ 2 □ 3 □ 4 □ 5 □ 10 □ More □
Trains?	1 □ 2 □ 3 □ 4 □ 5 □ 10 □ More □
Planes?	1 □ 2 □ 3 □ 4 □ 5 □ 10 □ More □

Who saw the first service station? _______________________________

Who saw the sea first? _______________________________

First asking to pee? _______________________________

First to say I'm hungry? _______________________________

First to say I'm thirsty? _______________________________

First to say *"Are we nearly there yet?"* _______________________________

Winner of dead lions? _______________________________

Who is in car?

____

____

____

Car colours:	Red ☐ Blue ☐ Green ☐ Yellow ☐
	Black ☐ White ☐ Silver ☐ Other ☐
Coaches?	1 ☐ 10 ☐ 20 ☐ 30 ☐ 40 ☐ 50 ☐ More ☐
Lorries?	1 ☐ 10 ☐ 20 ☐ 30 ☐ 40 ☐ 50 ☐ More ☐
Motor Bikes?	1 ☐ 10 ☐ 20 ☐ 30 ☐ 40 ☐ 50 ☐ More ☐
Caravans?	
Police Cars?	1 ☐ 2 ☐ 3 ☐ 4 ☐ 5 ☐ 10 ☐ More ☐
Cows?	1 ☐ 5 ☐ 10 ☐ 15 ☐ 20 ☐ 30 ☐ More ☐
Sheep?	1 ☐ 5 ☐ 10 ☐ 15 ☐ 20 ☐ 30 ☐ More ☐
Horses?	1 ☐ 5 ☐ 10 ☐ 15 ☐ 20 ☐ 30 ☐ More ☐
Windmills?	1 ☐ 2 ☐ 3 ☐ 4 ☐ 5 ☐ 10 ☐ More ☐
Trains?	1 ☐ 2 ☐ 3 ☐ 4 ☐ 5 ☐ 10 ☐ More ☐
Planes?	1 ☐ 2 ☐ 3 ☐ 4 ☐ 5 ☐ 10 ☐ More ☐
Who saw the first service station?	___________________________
Who saw the sea first?	___________________________
First asking to pee?	___________________________
First to say I'm hungry?	___________________________
First to say I'm thirsty?	___________________________
First to say *"Are we nearly there yet?"*	___________________________
Winner of dead lions?	___________________________

Who is in car?

____

____

____

Car colours:	Red □ Blue □ Green □ Yellow □
	Black □ White □ Silver □ Other □
Coaches?	1 □ 10 □ 20 □ 30 □ 40 □ 50 □ More □
Lorries?	1 □ 10 □ 20 □ 30 □ 40 □ 50 □ More □
Motor Bikes?	1 □ 10 □ 20 □ 30 □ 40 □ 50 □ More □
Caravans?	
Police Cars?	1 □ 2 □ 3 □ 4 □ 5 □ 10 □ More □
Cows?	1 □ 5 □ 10 □ 15 □ 20 □ 30 □ More □
Sheep?	1 □ 5 □ 10 □ 15 □ 20 □ 30 □ More □
Horses?	1 □ 5 □ 10 □ 15 □ 20 □ 30 □ More □
Windmills?	1 □ 2 □ 3 □ 4 □ 5 □ 10 □ More □
Trains?	1 □ 2 □ 3 □ 4 □ 5 □ 10 □ More □
Planes?	1 □ 2 □ 3 □ 4 □ 5 □ 10 □ More □

Who saw the first service station? _______________________________

Who saw the sea first? _______________________________

First asking to pee? _______________________________

First to say I'm hungry? _______________________________

First to say I'm thirsty? _______________________________

First to say *"Are we nearly there yet?"* _______________________________

Winner of dead lions? _______________________________

Who is in car?

____

____

____

Car colours:	Red □ Blue □ Green □ Yellow □
	Black □ White □ Silver □ Other □
Coaches?	1 □ 10 □ 20 □ 30 □ 40 □ 50 □ More □
Lorries?	1 □ 10 □ 20 □ 30 □ 40 □ 50 □ More □
Motor Bikes?	1 □ 10 □ 20 □ 30 □ 40 □ 50 □ More □
Caravans?	
Police Cars?	1 □ 2 □ 3 □ 4 □ 5 □ 10 □ More □
Cows?	1 □ 5 □ 10 □ 15 □ 20 □ 30 □ More □
Sheep?	1 □ 5 □ 10 □ 15 □ 20 □ 30 □ More □
Horses?	1 □ 5 □ 10 □ 15 □ 20 □ 30 □ More □
Windmills?	1 □ 2 □ 3 □ 4 □ 5 □ 10 □ More □
Trains?	1 □ 2 □ 3 □ 4 □ 5 □ 10 □ More □
Planes?	1 □ 2 □ 3 □ 4 □ 5 □ 10 □ More □
Who saw the first service station?	______________________________
Who saw the sea first?	______________________________
First asking to pee?	______________________________
First to say I'm hungry?	______________________________
First to say I'm thirsty?	______________________________
First to say *"Are we nearly there yet?"*	______________________________
Winner of dead lions?	______________________________

Who is in car?

____

____

____

Car colours:	Red ▢ Blue ▢ Green ▢ Yellow ▢ Black ▢ White ▢ Silver ▢ Other ▢
Coaches?	1 ▢ 10 ▢ 20 ▢ 30 ▢ 40 ▢ 50 ▢ More ▢
Lorries?	1 ▢ 10 ▢ 20 ▢ 30 ▢ 40 ▢ 50 ▢ More ▢
Motor Bikes?	1 ▢ 10 ▢ 20 ▢ 30 ▢ 40 ▢ 50 ▢ More ▢
Caravans?	
Police Cars?	1 ▢ 2 ▢ 3 ▢ 4 ▢ 5 ▢ 10 ▢ More ▢
Cows?	1 ▢ 5 ▢ 10 ▢ 15 ▢ 20 ▢ 30 ▢ More ▢
Sheep?	1 ▢ 5 ▢ 10 ▢ 15 ▢ 20 ▢ 30 ▢ More ▢
Horses?	1 ▢ 5 ▢ 10 ▢ 15 ▢ 20 ▢ 30 ▢ More ▢
Windmills?	1 ▢ 2 ▢ 3 ▢ 4 ▢ 5 ▢ 10 ▢ More ▢
Trains?	1 ▢ 2 ▢ 3 ▢ 4 ▢ 5 ▢ 10 ▢ More ▢
Planes?	1 ▢ 2 ▢ 3 ▢ 4 ▢ 5 ▢ 10 ▢ More ▢
Who saw the first service station?	____________________
Who saw the sea first?	____________________
First asking to pee?	____________________
First to say I'm hungry?	____________________
First to say I'm thirsty?	____________________
First to say *"Are we nearly there yet?"*	____________________
Winner of dead lions?	____________________

Who is in car?

____

____

____

Car colours:	Red ▢ Blue ▢ Green ▢ Yellow ▢
	Black ▢ White ▢ Silver ▢ Other ▢
Coaches?	1 ▢ 10 ▢ 20 ▢ 30 ▢ 40 ▢ 50 ▢ More ▢
Lorries?	1 ▢ 10 ▢ 20 ▢ 30 ▢ 40 ▢ 50 ▢ More ▢
Motor Bikes?	1 ▢ 10 ▢ 20 ▢ 30 ▢ 40 ▢ 50 ▢ More ▢
Caravans?	
Police Cars?	1 ▢ 2 ▢ 3 ▢ 4 ▢ 5 ▢ 10 ▢ More ▢
Cows?	1 ▢ 5 ▢ 10 ▢ 15 ▢ 20 ▢ 30 ▢ More ▢
Sheep?	1 ▢ 5 ▢ 10 ▢ 15 ▢ 20 ▢ 30 ▢ More ▢
Horses?	1 ▢ 5 ▢ 10 ▢ 15 ▢ 20 ▢ 30 ▢ More ▢
Windmills?	1 ▢ 2 ▢ 3 ▢ 4 ▢ 5 ▢ 10 ▢ More ▢
Trains?	1 ▢ 2 ▢ 3 ▢ 4 ▢ 5 ▢ 10 ▢ More ▢
Planes?	1 ▢ 2 ▢ 3 ▢ 4 ▢ 5 ▢ 10 ▢ More ▢
Who saw the first service station?	______________________
Who saw the sea first?	______________________
First asking to pee?	______________________
First to say I'm hungry?	______________________
First to say I'm thirsty?	______________________
First to say *"Are we nearly there yet?"*	______________________
Winner of dead lions?	______________________

Who is in car?

____

____

____

Car colours:	Red ☐ Blue ☐ Green ☐ Yellow ☐
	Black ☐ White ☐ Silver ☐ Other ☐
Coaches?	1 ☐ 10 ☐ 20 ☐ 30 ☐ 40 ☐ 50 ☐ More ☐
Lorries?	1 ☐ 10 ☐ 20 ☐ 30 ☐ 40 ☐ 50 ☐ More ☐
Motor Bikes?	1 ☐ 10 ☐ 20 ☐ 30 ☐ 40 ☐ 50 ☐ More ☐
Caravans?	
Police Cars?	1 ☐ 2 ☐ 3 ☐ 4 ☐ 5 ☐ 10 ☐ More ☐
Cows?	1 ☐ 5 ☐ 10 ☐ 15 ☐ 20 ☐ 30 ☐ More ☐
Sheep?	1 ☐ 5 ☐ 10 ☐ 15 ☐ 20 ☐ 30 ☐ More ☐
Horses?	1 ☐ 5 ☐ 10 ☐ 15 ☐ 20 ☐ 30 ☐ More ☐
Windmills?	1 ☐ 2 ☐ 3 ☐ 4 ☐ 5 ☐ 10 ☐ More ☐
Trains?	1 ☐ 2 ☐ 3 ☐ 4 ☐ 5 ☐ 10 ☐ More ☐
Planes?	1 ☐ 2 ☐ 3 ☐ 4 ☐ 5 ☐ 10 ☐ More ☐

Who saw the first service station? ______________________________

Who saw the sea first? ______________________________

First asking to pee? ______________________________

First to say I'm hungry? ______________________________

First to say I'm thirsty? ______________________________

First to say *"Are we nearly there yet?"* ______________________________

Winner of dead lions? ______________________________

Who is in car?

____

____

____

Car colours:	Red □ Blue □ Green □ Yellow □
	Black □ White □ Silver □ Other □
Coaches?	1 □ 10 □ 20 □ 30 □ 40 □ 50 □ More □
Lorries?	1 □ 10 □ 20 □ 30 □ 40 □ 50 □ More □
Motor Bikes?	1 □ 10 □ 20 □ 30 □ 40 □ 50 □ More □
Caravans?	
Police Cars?	1 □ 2 □ 3 □ 4 □ 5 □ 10 □ More □
Cows?	1 □ 5 □ 10 □ 15 □ 20 □ 30 □ More □
Sheep?	1 □ 5 □ 10 □ 15 □ 20 □ 30 □ More □
Horses?	1 □ 5 □ 10 □ 15 □ 20 □ 30 □ More □
Windmills?	1 □ 2 □ 3 □ 4 □ 5 □ 10 □ More □
Trains?	1 □ 2 □ 3 □ 4 □ 5 □ 10 □ More □
Planes?	1 □ 2 □ 3 □ 4 □ 5 □ 10 □ More □
Who saw the first service station?	_____________________
Who saw the sea first?	_____________________
First asking to pee?	_____________________
First to say I'm hungry?	_____________________
First to say I'm thirsty?	_____________________
First to say *"Are we nearly there yet?"*	_____________________
Winner of dead lions?	_____________________

Who is in car?

____

____

____

Car colours:	Red □ Blue □ Green □ Yellow □
	Black □ White □ Silver □ Other □
Coaches?	1 □ 10 □ 20 □ 30 □ 40 □ 50 □ More □
Lorries?	1 □ 10 □ 20 □ 30 □ 40 □ 50 □ More □
Motor Bikes?	1 □ 10 □ 20 □ 30 □ 40 □ 50 □ More □
Caravans?	
Police Cars?	1 □ 2 □ 3 □ 4 □ 5 □ 10 □ More □
Cows?	1 □ 5 □ 10 □ 15 □ 20 □ 30 □ More □
Sheep?	1 □ 5 □ 10 □ 15 □ 20 □ 30 □ More □
Horses?	1 □ 5 □ 10 □ 15 □ 20 □ 30 □ More □
Windmills?	1 □ 2 □ 3 □ 4 □ 5 □ 10 □ More □
Trains?	1 □ 2 □ 3 □ 4 □ 5 □ 10 □ More □
Planes?	1 □ 2 □ 3 □ 4 □ 5 □ 10 □ More □
Who saw the first service station?	_______________________
Who saw the sea first?	_______________________
First asking to pee?	_______________________
First to say I'm hungry?	_______________________
First to say I'm thirsty?	_______________________
First to say *"Are we nearly there yet?"*	_______________________
Winner of dead lions?	_______________________

Who is in car?

____

____

____

Car colours:	Red □ Blue □ Green □ Yellow □
	Black □ White □ Silver □ Other □
Coaches?	1 □ 10 □ 20 □ 30 □ 40 □ 50 □ More □
Lorries?	1 □ 10 □ 20 □ 30 □ 40 □ 50 □ More □
Motor Bikes?	1 □ 10 □ 20 □ 30 □ 40 □ 50 □ More □
Caravans?	
Police Cars?	1 □ 2 □ 3 □ 4 □ 5 □ 10 □ More □
Cows?	1 □ 5 □ 10 □ 15 □ 20 □ 30 □ More □
Sheep?	1 □ 5 □ 10 □ 15 □ 20 □ 30 □ More □
Horses?	1 □ 5 □ 10 □ 15 □ 20 □ 30 □ More □
Windmills?	1 □ 2 □ 3 □ 4 □ 5 □ 10 □ More □
Trains?	1 □ 2 □ 3 □ 4 □ 5 □ 10 □ More □
Planes?	1 □ 2 □ 3 □ 4 □ 5 □ 10 □ More □

Who saw the first service station?   ______________________________

Who saw the sea first?   ______________________________

First asking to pee?   ______________________________

First to say I'm hungry?   ______________________________

First to say I'm thirsty?   ______________________________

First to say *"Are we nearly there yet?"*   ______________________________

Winner of dead lions?   ______________________________

Who is in car?

____
____
____

Car colours:	Red □ Blue □ Green □ Yellow □
	Black □ White □ Silver □ Other □
Coaches?	1 □ 10 □ 20 □ 30 □ 40 □ 50 □ More □
Lorries?	1 □ 10 □ 20 □ 30 □ 40 □ 50 □ More □
Motor Bikes?	1 □ 10 □ 20 □ 30 □ 40 □ 50 □ More □
Caravans?	
Police Cars?	1 □ 2 □ 3 □ 4 □ 5 □ 10 □ More □
Cows?	1 □ 5 □ 10 □ 15 □ 20 □ 30 □ More □
Sheep?	1 □ 5 □ 10 □ 15 □ 20 □ 30 □ More □
Horses?	1 □ 5 □ 10 □ 15 □ 20 □ 30 □ More □
Windmills?	1 □ 2 □ 3 □ 4 □ 5 □ 10 □ More □
Trains?	1 □ 2 □ 3 □ 4 □ 5 □ 10 □ More □
Planes?	1 □ 2 □ 3 □ 4 □ 5 □ 10 □ More □

Who saw the first service station? _______________________

Who saw the sea first? _______________________

First asking to pee? _______________________

First to say I'm hungry? _______________________

First to say I'm thirsty? _______________________

First to say *"Are we nearly there yet?"* _______________________

Winner of dead lions? _______________________

Who is in car?

____
____
____

Car colours:	Red □ Blue □ Green □ Yellow □
	Black □ White □ Silver □ Other □
Coaches?	1 □ 10 □ 20 □ 30 □ 40 □ 50 □ More □
Lorries?	1 □ 10 □ 20 □ 30 □ 40 □ 50 □ More □
Motor Bikes?	1 □ 10 □ 20 □ 30 □ 40 □ 50 □ More □
Caravans?	
Police Cars?	1 □ 2 □ 3 □ 4 □ 5 □ 10 □ More □
Cows?	1 □ 5 □ 10 □ 15 □ 20 □ 30 □ More □
Sheep?	1 □ 5 □ 10 □ 15 □ 20 □ 30 □ More □
Horses?	1 □ 5 □ 10 □ 15 □ 20 □ 30 □ More □
Windmills?	1 □ 2 □ 3 □ 4 □ 5 □ 10 □ More □
Trains?	1 □ 2 □ 3 □ 4 □ 5 □ 10 □ More □
Planes?	1 □ 2 □ 3 □ 4 □ 5 □ 10 □ More □

Who saw the first service station? _______________________________

Who saw the sea first? _______________________________

First asking to pee? _______________________________

First to say I'm hungry? _______________________________

First to say I'm thirsty? _______________________________

First to say *"Are we nearly there yet?"* _______________________________

Winner of dead lions? _______________________________

Who is in car? _______________________
____
____

Car colours:	Red □ Blue □ Green □ Yellow □
	Black □ White □ Silver □ Other □
Coaches?	1 □ 10 □ 20 □ 30 □ 40 □ 50 □ More □
Lorries?	1 □ 10 □ 20 □ 30 □ 40 □ 50 □ More □
Motor Bikes?	1 □ 10 □ 20 □ 30 □ 40 □ 50 □ More □
Caravans?	
Police Cars?	1 □ 2 □ 3 □ 4 □ 5 □ 10 □ More □
Cows?	1 □ 5 □ 10 □ 15 □ 20 □ 30 □ More □
Sheep?	1 □ 5 □ 10 □ 15 □ 20 □ 30 □ More □
Horses?	1 □ 5 □ 10 □ 15 □ 20 □ 30 □ More □
Windmills?	1 □ 2 □ 3 □ 4 □ 5 □ 10 □ More □
Trains?	1 □ 2 □ 3 □ 4 □ 5 □ 10 □ More □
Planes?	1 □ 2 □ 3 □ 4 □ 5 □ 10 □ More □
Who saw the first service station?	_______________________
Who saw the sea first?	_______________________
First asking to pee?	_______________________
First to say I'm hungry?	_______________________
First to say I'm thirsty?	_______________________
First to say *"Are we nearly there yet?"*	_______________________
Winner of dead lions?	_______________________

Who is in car? ________________________
____
____

Car colours:	Red □ Blue □ Green □ Yellow □
	Black □ White □ Silver □ Other □
Coaches?	1 □ 10 □ 20 □ 30 □ 40 □ 50 □ More □
Lorries?	1 □ 10 □ 20 □ 30 □ 40 □ 50 □ More □
Motor Bikes?	1 □ 10 □ 20 □ 30 □ 40 □ 50 □ More □
Caravans?	
Police Cars?	1 □ 2 □ 3 □ 4 □ 5 □ 10 □ More □
Cows?	1 □ 5 □ 10 □ 15 □ 20 □ 30 □ More □
Sheep?	1 □ 5 □ 10 □ 15 □ 20 □ 30 □ More □
Horses?	1 □ 5 □ 10 □ 15 □ 20 □ 30 □ More □
Windmills?	1 □ 2 □ 3 □ 4 □ 5 □ 10 □ More □
Trains?	1 □ 2 □ 3 □ 4 □ 5 □ 10 □ More □
Planes?	1 □ 2 □ 3 □ 4 □ 5 □ 10 □ More □
Who saw the first service station?	________________________
Who saw the sea first?	________________________
First asking to pee?	________________________
First to say I'm hungry?	________________________
First to say I'm thirsty?	________________________
First to say *"Are we nearly there yet?"*	________________________
Winner of dead lions?	________________________

Who is in car? _______________________
____
____

Car colours:	Red □ Blue □ Green □ Yellow □
	Black □ White □ Silver □ Other □
Coaches?	1 □ 10 □ 20 □ 30 □ 40 □ 50 □ More □
Lorries?	1 □ 10 □ 20 □ 30 □ 40 □ 50 □ More □
Motor Bikes?	1 □ 10 □ 20 □ 30 □ 40 □ 50 □ More □
Caravans?	
Police Cars?	1 □ 2 □ 3 □ 4 □ 5 □ 10 □ More □
Cows?	1 □ 5 □ 10 □ 15 □ 20 □ 30 □ More □
Sheep?	1 □ 5 □ 10 □ 15 □ 20 □ 30 □ More □
Horses?	1 □ 5 □ 10 □ 15 □ 20 □ 30 □ More □
Windmills?	1 □ 2 □ 3 □ 4 □ 5 □ 10 □ More □
Trains?	1 □ 2 □ 3 □ 4 □ 5 □ 10 □ More □
Planes?	1 □ 2 □ 3 □ 4 □ 5 □ 10 □ More □
Who saw the first service station?	_______________________
Who saw the sea first?	_______________________
First asking to pee?	_______________________
First to say I'm hungry?	_______________________
First to say I'm thirsty?	_______________________
First to say *"Are we nearly there yet?"*	_______________________
Winner of dead lions?	_______________________

Who is in car?

____

____

____

Car colours: Red □ Blue □ Green □ Yellow □

Black □ White □ Silver □ Other □

Coaches?	1 □ 10 □ 20 □ 30 □ 40 □ 50 □ More □
Lorries?	1 □ 10 □ 20 □ 30 □ 40 □ 50 □ More □
Motor Bikes?	1 □ 10 □ 20 □ 30 □ 40 □ 50 □ More □
Caravans?	
Police Cars?	1 □ 2 □ 3 □ 4 □ 5 □ 10 □ More □
Cows?	1 □ 5 □ 10 □ 15 □ 20 □ 30 □ More □
Sheep?	1 □ 5 □ 10 □ 15 □ 20 □ 30 □ More □
Horses?	1 □ 5 □ 10 □ 15 □ 20 □ 30 □ More □
Windmills?	1 □ 2 □ 3 □ 4 □ 5 □ 10 □ More □
Trains?	1 □ 2 □ 3 □ 4 □ 5 □ 10 □ More □
Planes?	1 □ 2 □ 3 □ 4 □ 5 □ 10 □ More □

Who saw the first service station? _______________________________

Who saw the sea first? _______________________________

First asking to pee? _______________________________

First to say I'm hungry? _______________________________

First to say I'm thirsty? _______________________________

First to say *"Are we nearly there yet?"* _______________________________

Winner of dead lions? _______________________________

Who is in car? ______________________________
____
____

Car colours:	Red □ Blue □ Green □ Yellow □
	Black □ White □ Silver □ Other □
Coaches?	1 □ 10 □ 20 □ 30 □ 40 □ 50 □ More □
Lorries?	1 □ 10 □ 20 □ 30 □ 40 □ 50 □ More □
Motor Bikes?	1 □ 10 □ 20 □ 30 □ 40 □ 50 □ More □
Caravans?	
Police Cars?	1 □ 2 □ 3 □ 4 □ 5 □ 10 □ More □
Cows?	1 □ 5 □ 10 □ 15 □ 20 □ 30 □ More □
Sheep?	1 □ 5 □ 10 □ 15 □ 20 □ 30 □ More □
Horses?	1 □ 5 □ 10 □ 15 □ 20 □ 30 □ More □
Windmills?	1 □ 2 □ 3 □ 4 □ 5 □ 10 □ More □
Trains?	1 □ 2 □ 3 □ 4 □ 5 □ 10 □ More □
Planes?	1 □ 2 □ 3 □ 4 □ 5 □ 10 □ More □
Who saw the first service station?	______________________________
Who saw the sea first?	______________________________
First asking to pee?	______________________________
First to say I'm hungry?	______________________________
First to say I'm thirsty?	______________________________
First to say *"Are we nearly there yet?"*	______________________________
Winner of dead lions?	______________________________

Who is in car?

____

____

____

Car colours:	Red □ Blue □ Green □ Yellow □
	Black □ White □ Silver □ Other □

Coaches? 1 □ 10 □ 20 □ 30 □ 40 □ 50 □ More □

Lorries? 1 □ 10 □ 20 □ 30 □ 40 □ 50 □ More □

Motor Bikes? 1 □ 10 □ 20 □ 30 □ 40 □ 50 □ More □

Caravans?

Police Cars? 1 □ 2 □ 3 □ 4 □ 5 □ 10 □ More □

Cows? 1 □ 5 □ 10 □ 15 □ 20 □ 30 □ More □

Sheep? 1 □ 5 □ 10 □ 15 □ 20 □ 30 □ More □

Horses? 1 □ 5 □ 10 □ 15 □ 20 □ 30 □ More □

Windmills? 1 □ 2 □ 3 □ 4 □ 5 □ 10 □ More □

Trains? 1 □ 2 □ 3 □ 4 □ 5 □ 10 □ More □

Planes? 1 □ 2 □ 3 □ 4 □ 5 □ 10 □ More □

Who saw the first service station? _______________________________

Who saw the sea first? _______________________________

First asking to pee? _______________________________

First to say I'm hungry? _______________________________

First to say I'm thirsty? _______________________________

First to say *"Are we nearly there yet?"* _______________________________

Winner of dead lions? _______________________________

Who is in car? ___________________________
____
____

Car colours:	Red □ Blue □ Green □ Yellow □
	Black □ White □ Silver □ Other □
Coaches?	1 □ 10 □ 20 □ 30 □ 40 □ 50 □ More □
Lorries?	1 □ 10 □ 20 □ 30 □ 40 □ 50 □ More □
Motor Bikes?	1 □ 10 □ 20 □ 30 □ 40 □ 50 □ More □
Caravans?	
Police Cars?	1 □ 2 □ 3 □ 4 □ 5 □ 10 □ More □
Cows?	1 □ 5 □ 10 □ 15 □ 20 □ 30 □ More □
Sheep?	1 □ 5 □ 10 □ 15 □ 20 □ 30 □ More □
Horses?	1 □ 5 □ 10 □ 15 □ 20 □ 30 □ More □
Windmills?	1 □ 2 □ 3 □ 4 □ 5 □ 10 □ More □
Trains?	1 □ 2 □ 3 □ 4 □ 5 □ 10 □ More □
Planes?	1 □ 2 □ 3 □ 4 □ 5 □ 10 □ More □

Who saw the first service station? ___________________________

Who saw the sea first? ___________________________

First asking to pee? ___________________________

First to say I'm hungry? ___________________________

First to say I'm thirsty? ___________________________

First to say *"Are we nearly there yet?"* ___________________________

Winner of dead lions? ___________________________

Who is in car?

____

____

____

Car colours:	Red ☐ Blue ☐ Green ☐ Yellow ☐
	Black ☐ White ☐ Silver ☐ Other ☐
Coaches?	1 ☐ 10 ☐ 20 ☐ 30 ☐ 40 ☐ 50 ☐ More ☐
Lorries?	1 ☐ 10 ☐ 20 ☐ 30 ☐ 40 ☐ 50 ☐ More ☐
Motor Bikes?	1 ☐ 10 ☐ 20 ☐ 30 ☐ 40 ☐ 50 ☐ More ☐
Caravans?	
Police Cars?	1 ☐ 2 ☐ 3 ☐ 4 ☐ 5 ☐ 10 ☐ More ☐
Cows?	1 ☐ 5 ☐ 10 ☐ 15 ☐ 20 ☐ 30 ☐ More ☐
Sheep?	1 ☐ 5 ☐ 10 ☐ 15 ☐ 20 ☐ 30 ☐ More ☐
Horses?	1 ☐ 5 ☐ 10 ☐ 15 ☐ 20 ☐ 30 ☐ More ☐
Windmills?	1 ☐ 2 ☐ 3 ☐ 4 ☐ 5 ☐ 10 ☐ More ☐
Trains?	1 ☐ 2 ☐ 3 ☐ 4 ☐ 5 ☐ 10 ☐ More ☐
Planes?	1 ☐ 2 ☐ 3 ☐ 4 ☐ 5 ☐ 10 ☐ More ☐
Who saw the first service station?	_______________________
Who saw the sea first?	_______________________
First asking to pee?	_______________________
First to say I'm hungry?	_______________________
First to say I'm thirsty?	_______________________
First to say _"Are we nearly there yet?"_	_______________________
Winner of dead lions?	_______________________

Who is in car?

____

____

____

| Car colours: | Red □ Blue □ Green □ Yellow □ |
| | Black □ White □ Silver □ Other □ |

Coaches? 1 □ 10 □ 20 □ 30 □ 40 □ 50 □ More □

Lorries? 1 □ 10 □ 20 □ 30 □ 40 □ 50 □ More □

Motor Bikes? 1 □ 10 □ 20 □ 30 □ 40 □ 50 □ More □

Caravans?

Police Cars? 1 □ 2 □ 3 □ 4 □ 5 □ 10 □ More □

Cows? 1 □ 5 □ 10 □ 15 □ 20 □ 30 □ More □

Sheep? 1 □ 5 □ 10 □ 15 □ 20 □ 30 □ More □

Horses? 1 □ 5 □ 10 □ 15 □ 20 □ 30 □ More □

Windmills? 1 □ 2 □ 3 □ 4 □ 5 □ 10 □ More □

Trains? 1 □ 2 □ 3 □ 4 □ 5 □ 10 □ More □

Planes? 1 □ 2 □ 3 □ 4 □ 5 □ 10 □ More □

Who saw the first service station? _______________________________

Who saw the sea first? _______________________________

First asking to pee? _______________________________

First to say I'm hungry? _______________________________

First to say I'm thirsty? _______________________________

First to say *"Are we nearly there yet?"* _______________________________

Winner of dead lions? _______________________________

Who is in car?

____

____

____

Car colours:	Red □ Blue □ Green □ Yellow □
	Black □ White □ Silver □ Other □
Coaches?	1 □ 10 □ 20 □ 30 □ 40 □ 50 □ More □
Lorries?	1 □ 10 □ 20 □ 30 □ 40 □ 50 □ More □
Motor Bikes?	1 □ 10 □ 20 □ 30 □ 40 □ 50 □ More □
Caravans?	
Police Cars?	1 □ 2 □ 3 □ 4 □ 5 □ 10 □ More □
Cows?	1 □ 5 □ 10 □ 15 □ 20 □ 30 □ More □
Sheep?	1 □ 5 □ 10 □ 15 □ 20 □ 30 □ More □
Horses?	1 □ 5 □ 10 □ 15 □ 20 □ 30 □ More □
Windmills?	1 □ 2 □ 3 □ 4 □ 5 □ 10 □ More □
Trains?	1 □ 2 □ 3 □ 4 □ 5 □ 10 □ More □
Planes?	1 □ 2 □ 3 □ 4 □ 5 □ 10 □ More □

Who saw the first service station? ________________________________

Who saw the sea first? ________________________________

First asking to pee? ________________________________

First to say I'm hungry? ________________________________

First to say I'm thirsty? ________________________________

First to say *"Are we nearly there yet?"* ________________________________

Winner of dead lions? ________________________________

Who is in car? ______________________
____
____

Car colours:	Red □ Blue □ Green □ Yellow □
	Black □ White □ Silver □ Other □
Coaches?	1 □ 10 □ 20 □ 30 □ 40 □ 50 □ More □
Lorries?	1 □ 10 □ 20 □ 30 □ 40 □ 50 □ More □
Motor Bikes?	1 □ 10 □ 20 □ 30 □ 40 □ 50 □ More □
Caravans?	
Police Cars?	1 □ 2 □ 3 □ 4 □ 5 □ 10 □ More □
Cows?	1 □ 5 □ 10 □ 15 □ 20 □ 30 □ More □
Sheep?	1 □ 5 □ 10 □ 15 □ 20 □ 30 □ More □
Horses?	1 □ 5 □ 10 □ 15 □ 20 □ 30 □ More □
Windmills?	1 □ 2 □ 3 □ 4 □ 5 □ 10 □ More □
Trains?	1 □ 2 □ 3 □ 4 □ 5 □ 10 □ More □
Planes?	1 □ 2 □ 3 □ 4 □ 5 □ 10 □ More □
Who saw the first service station?	______________________
Who saw the sea first?	______________________
First asking to pee?	______________________
First to say I'm hungry?	______________________
First to say I'm thirsty?	______________________
First to say *"Are we nearly there yet?"*	______________________
Winner of dead lions?	______________________

Who is in car? _______________________________
____
____

Car colours:	Red □ Blue □ Green □ Yellow □ Black □ White □ Silver □ Other □
Coaches?	1 □ 10 □ 20 □ 30 □ 40 □ 50 □ More □
Lorries?	1 □ 10 □ 20 □ 30 □ 40 □ 50 □ More □
Motor Bikes?	1 □ 10 □ 20 □ 30 □ 40 □ 50 □ More □
Caravans?	
Police Cars?	1 □ 2 □ 3 □ 4 □ 5 □ 10 □ More □
Cows?	1 □ 5 □ 10 □ 15 □ 20 □ 30 □ More □
Sheep?	1 □ 5 □ 10 □ 15 □ 20 □ 30 □ More □
Horses?	1 □ 5 □ 10 □ 15 □ 20 □ 30 □ More □
Windmills?	1 □ 2 □ 3 □ 4 □ 5 □ 10 □ More □
Trains?	1 □ 2 □ 3 □ 4 □ 5 □ 10 □ More □
Planes?	1 □ 2 □ 3 □ 4 □ 5 □ 10 □ More □
Who saw the first service station?	___________________________
Who saw the sea first?	___________________________
First asking to pee?	___________________________
First to say I'm hungry?	___________________________
First to say I'm thirsty?	___________________________
First to say *"Are we nearly there yet?"*	___________________________
Winner of dead lions?	___________________________

Who is in car?

____

____

____

Car colours:	Red □ Blue □ Green □ Yellow □
	Black □ White □ Silver □ Other □
Coaches?	1 □ 10 □ 20 □ 30 □ 40 □ 50 □ More □
Lorries?	1 □ 10 □ 20 □ 30 □ 40 □ 50 □ More □
Motor Bikes?	1 □ 10 □ 20 □ 30 □ 40 □ 50 □ More □
Caravans?	
Police Cars?	1 □ 2 □ 3 □ 4 □ 5 □ 10 □ More □
Cows?	1 □ 5 □ 10 □ 15 □ 20 □ 30 □ More □
Sheep?	1 □ 5 □ 10 □ 15 □ 20 □ 30 □ More □
Horses?	1 □ 5 □ 10 □ 15 □ 20 □ 30 □ More □
Windmills?	1 □ 2 □ 3 □ 4 □ 5 □ 10 □ More □
Trains?	1 □ 2 □ 3 □ 4 □ 5 □ 10 □ More □
Planes?	1 □ 2 □ 3 □ 4 □ 5 □ 10 □ More □
Who saw the first service station?	_______________________
Who saw the sea first?	_______________________
First asking to pee?	_______________________
First to say I'm hungry?	_______________________
First to say I'm thirsty?	_______________________
First to say *"Are we nearly there yet?"*	_______________________
Winner of dead lions?	_______________________

Who is in car? ___________________

____

____

Car colours:	Red □ Blue □ Green □ Yellow □
	Black □ White □ Silver □ Other □
Coaches?	1 □ 10 □ 20 □ 30 □ 40 □ 50 □ More □
Lorries?	1 □ 10 □ 20 □ 30 □ 40 □ 50 □ More □
Motor Bikes?	1 □ 10 □ 20 □ 30 □ 40 □ 50 □ More □
Caravans?	
Police Cars?	1 □ 2 □ 3 □ 4 □ 5 □ 10 □ More □
Cows?	1 □ 5 □ 10 □ 15 □ 20 □ 30 □ More □
Sheep?	1 □ 5 □ 10 □ 15 □ 20 □ 30 □ More □
Horses?	1 □ 5 □ 10 □ 15 □ 20 □ 30 □ More □
Windmills?	1 □ 2 □ 3 □ 4 □ 5 □ 10 □ More □
Trains?	1 □ 2 □ 3 □ 4 □ 5 □ 10 □ More □
Planes?	1 □ 2 □ 3 □ 4 □ 5 □ 10 □ More □
Who saw the first service station?	_____________________
Who saw the sea first?	_____________________
First asking to pee?	_____________________
First to say I'm hungry?	_____________________
First to say I'm thirsty?	_____________________
First to say *"Are we nearly there yet?"*	_____________________
Winner of dead lions?	_____________________

Who is in car?

____

____

____

Car colours:	Red □ Blue □ Green □ Yellow □
	Black □ White □ Silver □ Other □
Coaches?	1 □ 10 □ 20 □ 30 □ 40 □ 50 □ More □
Lorries?	1 □ 10 □ 20 □ 30 □ 40 □ 50 □ More □
Motor Bikes?	1 □ 10 □ 20 □ 30 □ 40 □ 50 □ More □
Caravans?	
Police Cars?	1 □ 2 □ 3 □ 4 □ 5 □ 10 □ More □
Cows?	1 □ 5 □ 10 □ 15 □ 20 □ 30 □ More □
Sheep?	1 □ 5 □ 10 □ 15 □ 20 □ 30 □ More □
Horses?	1 □ 5 □ 10 □ 15 □ 20 □ 30 □ More □
Windmills?	1 □ 2 □ 3 □ 4 □ 5 □ 10 □ More □
Trains?	1 □ 2 □ 3 □ 4 □ 5 □ 10 □ More □
Planes?	1 □ 2 □ 3 □ 4 □ 5 □ 10 □ More □
Who saw the first service station?	____________________
Who saw the sea first?	____________________
First asking to pee?	____________________
First to say I'm hungry?	____________________
First to say I'm thirsty?	____________________
First to say *"Are we nearly there yet?"*	____________________
Winner of dead lions?	____________________

Who is in car?

____

____

____

Car colours:	Red □ Blue □ Green □ Yellow □
	Black □ White □ Silver □ Other □
Coaches?	1 □ 10 □ 20 □ 30 □ 40 □ 50 □ More □
Lorries?	1 □ 10 □ 20 □ 30 □ 40 □ 50 □ More □
Motor Bikes?	1 □ 10 □ 20 □ 30 □ 40 □ 50 □ More □
Caravans?	
Police Cars?	1 □ 2 □ 3 □ 4 □ 5 □ 10 □ More □
Cows?	1 □ 5 □ 10 □ 15 □ 20 □ 30 □ More □
Sheep?	1 □ 5 □ 10 □ 15 □ 20 □ 30 □ More □
Horses?	1 □ 5 □ 10 □ 15 □ 20 □ 30 □ More □
Windmills?	1 □ 2 □ 3 □ 4 □ 5 □ 10 □ More □
Trains?	1 □ 2 □ 3 □ 4 □ 5 □ 10 □ More □
Planes?	1 □ 2 □ 3 □ 4 □ 5 □ 10 □ More □

Who saw the first service station? _______________________________

Who saw the sea first? _______________________________

First asking to pee? _______________________________

First to say I'm hungry? _______________________________

First to say I'm thirsty? _______________________________

First to say *"Are we nearly there yet?"* _______________________________

Winner of dead lions? _______________________________

Who is in car?

____

____

____

Car colours:	Red ☐ Blue ☐ Green ☐ Yellow ☐ Black ☐ White ☐ Silver ☐ Other ☐
Coaches?	1 ☐ 10 ☐ 20 ☐ 30 ☐ 40 ☐ 50 ☐ More ☐
Lorries?	1 ☐ 10 ☐ 20 ☐ 30 ☐ 40 ☐ 50 ☐ More ☐
Motor Bikes?	1 ☐ 10 ☐ 20 ☐ 30 ☐ 40 ☐ 50 ☐ More ☐
Caravans?	
Police Cars?	1 ☐ 2 ☐ 3 ☐ 4 ☐ 5 ☐ 10 ☐ More ☐
Cows?	1 ☐ 5 ☐ 10 ☐ 15 ☐ 20 ☐ 30 ☐ More ☐
Sheep?	1 ☐ 5 ☐ 10 ☐ 15 ☐ 20 ☐ 30 ☐ More ☐
Horses?	1 ☐ 5 ☐ 10 ☐ 15 ☐ 20 ☐ 30 ☐ More ☐
Windmills?	1 ☐ 2 ☐ 3 ☐ 4 ☐ 5 ☐ 10 ☐ More ☐
Trains?	1 ☐ 2 ☐ 3 ☐ 4 ☐ 5 ☐ 10 ☐ More ☐
Planes?	1 ☐ 2 ☐ 3 ☐ 4 ☐ 5 ☐ 10 ☐ More ☐
Who saw the first service station?	_____________________
Who saw the sea first?	_____________________
First asking to pee?	_____________________
First to say I'm hungry?	_____________________
First to say I'm thirsty?	_____________________
First to say *"Are we nearly there yet?"*	_____________________
Winner of dead lions?	_____________________

Who is in car?

____
____
____

Car colours:	Red □ Blue □ Green □ Yellow □ Black □ White □ Silver □ Other □
Coaches?	1 □ 10 □ 20 □ 30 □ 40 □ 50 □ More □
Lorries?	1 □ 10 □ 20 □ 30 □ 40 □ 50 □ More □
Motor Bikes?	1 □ 10 □ 20 □ 30 □ 40 □ 50 □ More □
Caravans?	
Police Cars?	1 □ 2 □ 3 □ 4 □ 5 □ 10 □ More □
Cows?	1 □ 5 □ 10 □ 15 □ 20 □ 30 □ More □
Sheep?	1 □ 5 □ 10 □ 15 □ 20 □ 30 □ More □
Horses?	1 □ 5 □ 10 □ 15 □ 20 □ 30 □ More □
Windmills?	1 □ 2 □ 3 □ 4 □ 5 □ 10 □ More □
Trains?	1 □ 2 □ 3 □ 4 □ 5 □ 10 □ More □
Planes?	1 □ 2 □ 3 □ 4 □ 5 □ 10 □ More □
Who saw the first service station?	_______________________
Who saw the sea first?	_______________________
First asking to pee?	_______________________
First to say I'm hungry?	_______________________
First to say I'm thirsty?	_______________________
First to say *"Are we nearly there yet?"*	_______________________
Winner of dead lions?	_______________________

Who is in car?

____

____

____

Car colours:	Red □ Blue □ Green □ Yellow □
	Black □ White □ Silver □ Other □
Coaches?	1 □ 10 □ 20 □ 30 □ 40 □ 50 □ More □
Lorries?	1 □ 10 □ 20 □ 30 □ 40 □ 50 □ More □
Motor Bikes?	1 □ 10 □ 20 □ 30 □ 40 □ 50 □ More □
Caravans?	
Police Cars?	1 □ 2 □ 3 □ 4 □ 5 □ 10 □ More □
Cows?	1 □ 5 □ 10 □ 15 □ 20 □ 30 □ More □
Sheep?	1 □ 5 □ 10 □ 15 □ 20 □ 30 □ More □
Horses?	1 □ 5 □ 10 □ 15 □ 20 □ 30 □ More □
Windmills?	1 □ 2 □ 3 □ 4 □ 5 □ 10 □ More □
Trains?	1 □ 2 □ 3 □ 4 □ 5 □ 10 □ More □
Planes?	1 □ 2 □ 3 □ 4 □ 5 □ 10 □ More □

Who saw the first service station? _______________________________

Who saw the sea first? _______________________________

First asking to pee? _______________________________

First to say I'm hungry? _______________________________

First to say I'm thirsty? _______________________________

First to say *"Are we nearly there yet?"* _______________________________

Winner of dead lions? _______________________________

<table>
<tr><td>

Who is in car?

</td><td>

____

____

____

</td></tr>
</table>

Car colours:	Red □ Blue □ Green □ Yellow □
	Black □ White □ Silver □ Other □
Coaches?	1 □ 10 □ 20 □ 30 □ 40 □ 50 □ More □
Lorries?	1 □ 10 □ 20 □ 30 □ 40 □ 50 □ More □
Motor Bikes?	1 □ 10 □ 20 □ 30 □ 40 □ 50 □ More □
Caravans?	
Police Cars?	1 □ 2 □ 3 □ 4 □ 5 □ 10 □ More □
Cows?	1 □ 5 □ 10 □ 15 □ 20 □ 30 □ More □
Sheep?	1 □ 5 □ 10 □ 15 □ 20 □ 30 □ More □
Horses?	1 □ 5 □ 10 □ 15 □ 20 □ 30 □ More □
Windmills?	1 □ 2 □ 3 □ 4 □ 5 □ 10 □ More □
Trains?	1 □ 2 □ 3 □ 4 □ 5 □ 10 □ More □
Planes?	1 □ 2 □ 3 □ 4 □ 5 □ 10 □ More □
Who saw the first service station?	_______________________________
Who saw the sea first?	_______________________________
First asking to pee?	_______________________________
First to say I'm hungry?	_______________________________
First to say I'm thirsty?	_______________________________
First to say _"Are we nearly there yet?"_	_______________________________
Winner of dead lions?	_______________________________

Who is in car?

____

____

____

Car colours:	Red □ Blue □ Green □ Yellow □
	Black □ White □ Silver □ Other □
Coaches?	1 □ 10 □ 20 □ 30 □ 40 □ 50 □ More □
Lorries?	1 □ 10 □ 20 □ 30 □ 40 □ 50 □ More □
Motor Bikes?	1 □ 10 □ 20 □ 30 □ 40 □ 50 □ More □
Caravans?	
Police Cars?	1 □ 2 □ 3 □ 4 □ 5 □ 10 □ More □
Cows?	1 □ 5 □ 10 □ 15 □ 20 □ 30 □ More □
Sheep?	1 □ 5 □ 10 □ 15 □ 20 □ 30 □ More □
Horses?	1 □ 5 □ 10 □ 15 □ 20 □ 30 □ More □
Windmills?	1 □ 2 □ 3 □ 4 □ 5 □ 10 □ More □
Trains?	1 □ 2 □ 3 □ 4 □ 5 □ 10 □ More □
Planes?	1 □ 2 □ 3 □ 4 □ 5 □ 10 □ More □

Who saw the first service station? _______________________________

Who saw the sea first? _______________________________

First asking to pee? _______________________________

First to say I'm hungry? _______________________________

First to say I'm thirsty? _______________________________

First to say *"Are we nearly there yet?"* _______________________________

Winner of dead lions? _______________________________

Who is in car? ____________________

____

____

Car colours:	Red □ Blue □ Green □ Yellow □
	Black □ White □ Silver □ Other □
Coaches?	1 □ 10 □ 20 □ 30 □ 40 □ 50 □ More □
Lorries?	1 □ 10 □ 20 □ 30 □ 40 □ 50 □ More □
Motor Bikes?	1 □ 10 □ 20 □ 30 □ 40 □ 50 □ More □
Caravans?	
Police Cars?	1 □ 2 □ 3 □ 4 □ 5 □ 10 □ More □
Cows?	1 □ 5 □ 10 □ 15 □ 20 □ 30 □ More □
Sheep?	1 □ 5 □ 10 □ 15 □ 20 □ 30 □ More □
Horses?	1 □ 5 □ 10 □ 15 □ 20 □ 30 □ More □
Windmills?	1 □ 2 □ 3 □ 4 □ 5 □ 10 □ More □
Trains?	1 □ 2 □ 3 □ 4 □ 5 □ 10 □ More □
Planes?	1 □ 2 □ 3 □ 4 □ 5 □ 10 □ More □
Who saw the first service station?	__________________
Who saw the sea first?	__________________
First asking to pee?	__________________
First to say I'm hungry?	__________________
First to say I'm thirsty?	__________________
First to say *"Are we nearly there yet?"*	__________________
Winner of dead lions?	__________________

Who is in car?

____

____

____

Car colours:	Red □ Blue □ Green □ Yellow □
	Black □ White □ Silver □ Other □
Coaches?	1 □ 10 □ 20 □ 30 □ 40 □ 50 □ More □
Lorries?	1 □ 10 □ 20 □ 30 □ 40 □ 50 □ More □
Motor Bikes?	1 □ 10 □ 20 □ 30 □ 40 □ 50 □ More □
Caravans?	
Police Cars?	1 □ 2 □ 3 □ 4 □ 5 □ 10 □ More □
Cows?	1 □ 5 □ 10 □ 15 □ 20 □ 30 □ More □
Sheep?	1 □ 5 □ 10 □ 15 □ 20 □ 30 □ More □
Horses?	1 □ 5 □ 10 □ 15 □ 20 □ 30 □ More □
Windmills?	1 □ 2 □ 3 □ 4 □ 5 □ 10 □ More □
Trains?	1 □ 2 □ 3 □ 4 □ 5 □ 10 □ More □
Planes?	1 □ 2 □ 3 □ 4 □ 5 □ 10 □ More □

Who saw the first service station? _______________________________

Who saw the sea first? _______________________________

First asking to pee? _______________________________

First to say I'm hungry? _______________________________

First to say I'm thirsty? _______________________________

First to say *"Are we nearly there yet?"* _______________________________

Winner of dead lions? _______________________________

Who is in car?

____

____

____

| Car colours: | Red □ Blue □ Green □ Yellow □ |
| | Black □ White □ Silver □ Other □ |

Coaches? — 1 □ 10 □ 20 □ 30 □ 40 □ 50 □ More □

Lorries? — 1 □ 10 □ 20 □ 30 □ 40 □ 50 □ More □

Motor Bikes? — 1 □ 10 □ 20 □ 30 □ 40 □ 50 □ More □

Caravans?

Police Cars? — 1 □ 2 □ 3 □ 4 □ 5 □ 10 □ More □

Cows? — 1 □ 5 □ 10 □ 15 □ 20 □ 30 □ More □

Sheep? — 1 □ 5 □ 10 □ 15 □ 20 □ 30 □ More □

Horses? — 1 □ 5 □ 10 □ 15 □ 20 □ 30 □ More □

Windmills? — 1 □ 2 □ 3 □ 4 □ 5 □ 10 □ More □

Trains? — 1 □ 2 □ 3 □ 4 □ 5 □ 10 □ More □

Planes? — 1 □ 2 □ 3 □ 4 □ 5 □ 10 □ More □

Who saw the first service station? _______________________

Who saw the sea first? _______________________

First asking to pee? _______________________

First to say I'm hungry? _______________________

First to say I'm thirsty? _______________________

First to say *"Are we nearly there yet?"* _______________________

Winner of dead lions? _______________________

Who is in car? _______________________________

____

____

Car colours:	Red ☐ Blue ☐ Green ☐ Yellow ☐
	Black ☐ White ☐ Silver ☐ Other ☐
Coaches?	1 ☐ 10 ☐ 20 ☐ 30 ☐ 40 ☐ 50 ☐ More ☐
Lorries?	1 ☐ 10 ☐ 20 ☐ 30 ☐ 40 ☐ 50 ☐ More ☐
Motor Bikes?	1 ☐ 10 ☐ 20 ☐ 30 ☐ 40 ☐ 50 ☐ More ☐
Caravans?	
Police Cars?	1 ☐ 2 ☐ 3 ☐ 4 ☐ 5 ☐ 10 ☐ More ☐
Cows?	1 ☐ 5 ☐ 10 ☐ 15 ☐ 20 ☐ 30 ☐ More ☐
Sheep?	1 ☐ 5 ☐ 10 ☐ 15 ☐ 20 ☐ 30 ☐ More ☐
Horses?	1 ☐ 5 ☐ 10 ☐ 15 ☐ 20 ☐ 30 ☐ More ☐
Windmills?	1 ☐ 2 ☐ 3 ☐ 4 ☐ 5 ☐ 10 ☐ More ☐
Trains?	1 ☐ 2 ☐ 3 ☐ 4 ☐ 5 ☐ 10 ☐ More ☐
Planes?	1 ☐ 2 ☐ 3 ☐ 4 ☐ 5 ☐ 10 ☐ More ☐
Who saw the first service station?	_______________________
Who saw the sea first?	_______________________
First asking to pee?	_______________________
First to say I'm hungry?	_______________________
First to say I'm thirsty?	_______________________
First to say *"Are we nearly there yet?"*	_______________________
Winner of dead lions?	_______________________

Who is in car?

____
____
____

Car colours:	Red □ Blue □ Green □ Yellow □
	Black □ White □ Silver □ Other □
Coaches?	1 □ 10 □ 20 □ 30 □ 40 □ 50 □ More □
Lorries?	1 □ 10 □ 20 □ 30 □ 40 □ 50 □ More □
Motor Bikes?	1 □ 10 □ 20 □ 30 □ 40 □ 50 □ More □
Caravans?	
Police Cars?	1 □ 2 □ 3 □ 4 □ 5 □ 10 □ More □
Cows?	1 □ 5 □ 10 □ 15 □ 20 □ 30 □ More □
Sheep?	1 □ 5 □ 10 □ 15 □ 20 □ 30 □ More □
Horses?	1 □ 5 □ 10 □ 15 □ 20 □ 30 □ More □
Windmills?	1 □ 2 □ 3 □ 4 □ 5 □ 10 □ More □
Trains?	1 □ 2 □ 3 □ 4 □ 5 □ 10 □ More □
Planes?	1 □ 2 □ 3 □ 4 □ 5 □ 10 □ More □
Who saw the first service station?	______________________________
Who saw the sea first?	______________________________
First asking to pee?	______________________________
First to say I'm hungry?	______________________________
First to say I'm thirsty?	______________________________
First to say _"Are we nearly there yet?"_	______________________________
Winner of dead lions?	______________________________

Who is in car?

____

____

____

Car colours:	Red □ Blue □ Green □ Yellow □
	Black □ White □ Silver □ Other □
Coaches?	1 □ 10 □ 20 □ 30 □ 40 □ 50 □ More □
Lorries?	1 □ 10 □ 20 □ 30 □ 40 □ 50 □ More □
Motor Bikes?	1 □ 10 □ 20 □ 30 □ 40 □ 50 □ More □
Caravans?	
Police Cars?	1 □ 2 □ 3 □ 4 □ 5 □ 10 □ More □
Cows?	1 □ 5 □ 10 □ 15 □ 20 □ 30 □ More □
Sheep?	1 □ 5 □ 10 □ 15 □ 20 □ 30 □ More □
Horses?	1 □ 5 □ 10 □ 15 □ 20 □ 30 □ More □
Windmills?	1 □ 2 □ 3 □ 4 □ 5 □ 10 □ More □
Trains?	1 □ 2 □ 3 □ 4 □ 5 □ 10 □ More □
Planes?	1 □ 2 □ 3 □ 4 □ 5 □ 10 □ More □

Who saw the first service station? _____________________________

Who saw the sea first? _____________________________

First asking to pee? _____________________________

First to say I'm hungry? _____________________________

First to say I'm thirsty? _____________________________

First to say *"Are we nearly there yet?"* _____________________________

Winner of dead lions? _____________________________

Who is in car? _______________________

____

____

Car colours:	Red ☐ Blue ☐ Green ☐ Yellow ☐
	Black ☐ White ☐ Silver ☐ Other ☐
Coaches?	1 ☐ 10 ☐ 20 ☐ 30 ☐ 40 ☐ 50 ☐ More ☐
Lorries?	1 ☐ 10 ☐ 20 ☐ 30 ☐ 40 ☐ 50 ☐ More ☐
Motor Bikes?	1 ☐ 10 ☐ 20 ☐ 30 ☐ 40 ☐ 50 ☐ More ☐
Caravans?	
Police Cars?	1 ☐ 2 ☐ 3 ☐ 4 ☐ 5 ☐ 10 ☐ More ☐
Cows?	1 ☐ 5 ☐ 10 ☐ 15 ☐ 20 ☐ 30 ☐ More ☐
Sheep?	1 ☐ 5 ☐ 10 ☐ 15 ☐ 20 ☐ 30 ☐ More ☐
Horses?	1 ☐ 5 ☐ 10 ☐ 15 ☐ 20 ☐ 30 ☐ More ☐
Windmills?	1 ☐ 2 ☐ 3 ☐ 4 ☐ 5 ☐ 10 ☐ More ☐
Trains?	1 ☐ 2 ☐ 3 ☐ 4 ☐ 5 ☐ 10 ☐ More ☐
Planes?	1 ☐ 2 ☐ 3 ☐ 4 ☐ 5 ☐ 10 ☐ More ☐
Who saw the first service station?	_______________________
Who saw the sea first?	_______________________
First asking to pee?	_______________________
First to say I'm hungry?	_______________________
First to say I'm thirsty?	_______________________
First to say *"Are we nearly there yet?"*	_______________________
Winner of dead lions?	_______________________

Who is in car? __________________________
____
____

Car colours:	Red ☐ Blue ☐ Green ☐ Yellow ☐
	Black ☐ White ☐ Silver ☐ Other ☐
Coaches?	1 ☐ 10 ☐ 20 ☐ 30 ☐ 40 ☐ 50 ☐ More ☐
Lorries?	1 ☐ 10 ☐ 20 ☐ 30 ☐ 40 ☐ 50 ☐ More ☐
Motor Bikes?	1 ☐ 10 ☐ 20 ☐ 30 ☐ 40 ☐ 50 ☐ More ☐
Caravans?	
Police Cars?	1 ☐ 2 ☐ 3 ☐ 4 ☐ 5 ☐ 10 ☐ More ☐
Cows?	1 ☐ 5 ☐ 10 ☐ 15 ☐ 20 ☐ 30 ☐ More ☐
Sheep?	1 ☐ 5 ☐ 10 ☐ 15 ☐ 20 ☐ 30 ☐ More ☐
Horses?	1 ☐ 5 ☐ 10 ☐ 15 ☐ 20 ☐ 30 ☐ More ☐
Windmills?	1 ☐ 2 ☐ 3 ☐ 4 ☐ 5 ☐ 10 ☐ More ☐
Trains?	1 ☐ 2 ☐ 3 ☐ 4 ☐ 5 ☐ 10 ☐ More ☐
Planes?	1 ☐ 2 ☐ 3 ☐ 4 ☐ 5 ☐ 10 ☐ More ☐
Who saw the first service station?	_______________________
Who saw the sea first?	_______________________
First asking to pee?	_______________________
First to say I'm hungry?	_______________________
First to say I'm thirsty?	_______________________
First to say *"Are we nearly there yet?"*	_______________________
Winner of dead lions?	_______________________

Who is in car?

____

____

____

Car colours:	Red □ Blue □ Green □ Yellow □
	Black □ White □ Silver □ Other □
Coaches?	1 □ 10 □ 20 □ 30 □ 40 □ 50 □ More □
Lorries?	1 □ 10 □ 20 □ 30 □ 40 □ 50 □ More □
Motor Bikes?	1 □ 10 □ 20 □ 30 □ 40 □ 50 □ More □
Caravans?	
Police Cars?	1 □ 2 □ 3 □ 4 □ 5 □ 10 □ More □
Cows?	1 □ 5 □ 10 □ 15 □ 20 □ 30 □ More □
Sheep?	1 □ 5 □ 10 □ 15 □ 20 □ 30 □ More □
Horses?	1 □ 5 □ 10 □ 15 □ 20 □ 30 □ More □
Windmills?	1 □ 2 □ 3 □ 4 □ 5 □ 10 □ More □
Trains?	1 □ 2 □ 3 □ 4 □ 5 □ 10 □ More □
Planes?	1 □ 2 □ 3 □ 4 □ 5 □ 10 □ More □

Who saw the first service station? _______________________________

Who saw the sea first? _______________________________

First asking to pee? _______________________________

First to say I'm hungry? _______________________________

First to say I'm thirsty? _______________________________

First to say *"Are we nearly there yet?"* _______________________________

Winner of dead lions? _______________________________

Who is in car? _______________________________
____
____

Car colours:	Red □ Blue □ Green □ Yellow □
	Black □ White □ Silver □ Other □
Coaches?	1 □ 10 □ 20 □ 30 □ 40 □ 50 □ More □
Lorries?	1 □ 10 □ 20 □ 30 □ 40 □ 50 □ More □
Motor Bikes?	1 □ 10 □ 20 □ 30 □ 40 □ 50 □ More □
Caravans?	
Police Cars?	1 □ 2 □ 3 □ 4 □ 5 □ 10 □ More □
Cows?	1 □ 5 □ 10 □ 15 □ 20 □ 30 □ More □
Sheep?	1 □ 5 □ 10 □ 15 □ 20 □ 30 □ More □
Horses?	1 □ 5 □ 10 □ 15 □ 20 □ 30 □ More □
Windmills?	1 □ 2 □ 3 □ 4 □ 5 □ 10 □ More □
Trains?	1 □ 2 □ 3 □ 4 □ 5 □ 10 □ More □
Planes?	1 □ 2 □ 3 □ 4 □ 5 □ 10 □ More □
Who saw the first service station?	_______________________
Who saw the sea first?	_______________________
First asking to pee?	_______________________
First to say I'm hungry?	_______________________
First to say I'm thirsty?	_______________________
First to say *"Are we nearly there yet?"*	_______________________
Winner of dead lions?	_______________________

Who is in car?

____
____
____

Car colours: Red □ Blue □ Green □ Yellow □

Black □ White □ Silver □ Other □

Coaches?   1 □ 10 □ 20 □ 30 □ 40 □ 50 □ More □

Lorries?   1 □ 10 □ 20 □ 30 □ 40 □ 50 □ More □

Motor Bikes?   1 □ 10 □ 20 □ 30 □ 40 □ 50 □ More □

Caravans?

Police Cars?   1 □ 2 □ 3 □ 4 □ 5 □ 10 □ More □

Cows?   1 □ 5 □ 10 □ 15 □ 20 □ 30 □ More □

Sheep?   1 □ 5 □ 10 □ 15 □ 20 □ 30 □ More □

Horses?   1 □ 5 □ 10 □ 15 □ 20 □ 30 □ More □

Windmills?   1 □ 2 □ 3 □ 4 □ 5 □ 10 □ More □

Trains?   1 □ 2 □ 3 □ 4 □ 5 □ 10 □ More □

Planes?   1 □ 2 □ 3 □ 4 □ 5 □ 10 □ More □

Who saw the first service   _______________________________
station?

Who saw the sea first?   _______________________________

First asking to pee?   _______________________________

First to say I'm hungry?   _______________________________

First to say I'm thirsty?   _______________________________

First to say *"Are we nearly* _______________________________
there yet?"

Winner of dead lions?   _______________________________

Who is in car? _______________________________
____
____

Car colours:	Red □ Blue □ Green □ Yellow □
	Black □ White □ Silver □ Other □
Coaches?	1 □ 10 □ 20 □ 30 □ 40 □ 50 □ More □
Lorries?	1 □ 10 □ 20 □ 30 □ 40 □ 50 □ More □
Motor Bikes?	1 □ 10 □ 20 □ 30 □ 40 □ 50 □ More □
Caravans?	
Police Cars?	1 □ 2 □ 3 □ 4 □ 5 □ 10 □ More □
Cows?	1 □ 5 □ 10 □ 15 □ 20 □ 30 □ More □
Sheep?	1 □ 5 □ 10 □ 15 □ 20 □ 30 □ More □
Horses?	1 □ 5 □ 10 □ 15 □ 20 □ 30 □ More □
Windmills?	1 □ 2 □ 3 □ 4 □ 5 □ 10 □ More □
Trains?	1 □ 2 □ 3 □ 4 □ 5 □ 10 □ More □
Planes?	1 □ 2 □ 3 □ 4 □ 5 □ 10 □ More □
Who saw the first service station?	_______________________
Who saw the sea first?	_______________________
First asking to pee?	_______________________
First to say I'm hungry?	_______________________
First to say I'm thirsty?	_______________________
First to say *"Are we nearly there yet?"*	_______________________
Winner of dead lions?	_______________________

Who is in car?

____

____

____

Car colours:	Red □ Blue □ Green □ Yellow □
	Black □ White □ Silver □ Other □
Coaches?	1 □ 10 □ 20 □ 30 □ 40 □ 50 □ More □
Lorries?	1 □ 10 □ 20 □ 30 □ 40 □ 50 □ More □
Motor Bikes?	1 □ 10 □ 20 □ 30 □ 40 □ 50 □ More □
Caravans?	
Police Cars?	1 □ 2 □ 3 □ 4 □ 5 □ 10 □ More □
Cows?	1 □ 5 □ 10 □ 15 □ 20 □ 30 □ More □
Sheep?	1 □ 5 □ 10 □ 15 □ 20 □ 30 □ More □
Horses?	1 □ 5 □ 10 □ 15 □ 20 □ 30 □ More □
Windmills?	1 □ 2 □ 3 □ 4 □ 5 □ 10 □ More □
Trains?	1 □ 2 □ 3 □ 4 □ 5 □ 10 □ More □
Planes?	1 □ 2 □ 3 □ 4 □ 5 □ 10 □ More □

Who saw the first service station? ______________________________

Who saw the sea first? ______________________________

First asking to pee? ______________________________

First to say I'm hungry? ______________________________

First to say I'm thirsty? ______________________________

First to say *"Are we nearly there yet?"* ______________________________

Winner of dead lions? ______________________________

Who is in car?   ______________________
____
____

Car colours:	Red □ Blue □ Green □ Yellow □ Black □ White □ Silver □ Other □
Coaches?	1 □ 10 □ 20 □ 30 □ 40 □ 50 □ More □
Lorries?	1 □ 10 □ 20 □ 30 □ 40 □ 50 □ More □
Motor Bikes?	1 □ 10 □ 20 □ 30 □ 40 □ 50 □ More □
Caravans?	
Police Cars?	1 □ 2 □ 3 □ 4 □ 5 □ 10 □ More □
Cows?	1 □ 5 □ 10 □ 15 □ 20 □ 30 □ More □
Sheep?	1 □ 5 □ 10 □ 15 □ 20 □ 30 □ More □
Horses?	1 □ 5 □ 10 □ 15 □ 20 □ 30 □ More □
Windmills?	1 □ 2 □ 3 □ 4 □ 5 □ 10 □ More □
Trains?	1 □ 2 □ 3 □ 4 □ 5 □ 10 □ More □
Planes?	1 □ 2 □ 3 □ 4 □ 5 □ 10 □ More □
Who saw the first service station?	______________________
Who saw the sea first?	______________________
First asking to pee?	______________________
First to say I'm hungry?	______________________
First to say I'm thirsty?	______________________
First to say *"Are we nearly there yet?"*	______________________
Winner of dead lions?	______________________

Who is in car?

____
____
____

Car colours:	Red ◻ Blue ◻ Green ◻ Yellow ◻
	Black ◻ White ◻ Silver ◻ Other ◻
Coaches?	1 ◻ 10 ◻ 20 ◻ 30 ◻ 40 ◻ 50 ◻ More ◻
Lorries?	1 ◻ 10 ◻ 20 ◻ 30 ◻ 40 ◻ 50 ◻ More ◻
Motor Bikes?	1 ◻ 10 ◻ 20 ◻ 30 ◻ 40 ◻ 50 ◻ More ◻
Caravans?	
Police Cars?	1 ◻ 2 ◻ 3 ◻ 4 ◻ 5 ◻ 10 ◻ More ◻
Cows?	1 ◻ 5 ◻ 10 ◻ 15 ◻ 20 ◻ 30 ◻ More ◻
Sheep?	1 ◻ 5 ◻ 10 ◻ 15 ◻ 20 ◻ 30 ◻ More ◻
Horses?	1 ◻ 5 ◻ 10 ◻ 15 ◻ 20 ◻ 30 ◻ More ◻
Windmills?	1 ◻ 2 ◻ 3 ◻ 4 ◻ 5 ◻ 10 ◻ More ◻
Trains?	1 ◻ 2 ◻ 3 ◻ 4 ◻ 5 ◻ 10 ◻ More ◻
Planes?	1 ◻ 2 ◻ 3 ◻ 4 ◻ 5 ◻ 10 ◻ More ◻
Who saw the first service station?	_____________________
Who saw the sea first?	_____________________
First asking to pee?	_____________________
First to say I'm hungry?	_____________________
First to say I'm thirsty?	_____________________
First to say _"Are we nearly there yet?"_	_____________________
Winner of dead lions?	_____________________

Who is in car?

____

____

____

Car colours:	Red □ Blue □ Green □ Yellow □ Black □ White □ Silver □ Other □
Coaches?	1 □ 10 □ 20 □ 30 □ 40 □ 50 □ More □
Lorries?	1 □ 10 □ 20 □ 30 □ 40 □ 50 □ More □
Motor Bikes?	1 □ 10 □ 20 □ 30 □ 40 □ 50 □ More □
Caravans?	
Police Cars?	1 □ 2 □ 3 □ 4 □ 5 □ 10 □ More □
Cows?	1 □ 5 □ 10 □ 15 □ 20 □ 30 □ More □
Sheep?	1 □ 5 □ 10 □ 15 □ 20 □ 30 □ More □
Horses?	1 □ 5 □ 10 □ 15 □ 20 □ 30 □ More □
Windmills?	1 □ 2 □ 3 □ 4 □ 5 □ 10 □ More □
Trains?	1 □ 2 □ 3 □ 4 □ 5 □ 10 □ More □
Planes?	1 □ 2 □ 3 □ 4 □ 5 □ 10 □ More □
Who saw the first service station?	_______________________
Who saw the sea first?	_______________________
First asking to pee?	_______________________
First to say I'm hungry?	_______________________
First to say I'm thirsty?	_______________________
First to say *"Are we nearly there yet?"*	_______________________
Winner of dead lions?	_______________________

Who is in car?

____

____

____

Car colours:	Red □ Blue □ Green □ Yellow □
	Black □ White □ Silver □ Other □
Coaches?	1 □ 10 □ 20 □ 30 □ 40 □ 50 □ More □
Lorries?	1 □ 10 □ 20 □ 30 □ 40 □ 50 □ More □
Motor Bikes?	1 □ 10 □ 20 □ 30 □ 40 □ 50 □ More □
Caravans?	
Police Cars?	1 □ 2 □ 3 □ 4 □ 5 □ 10 □ More □
Cows?	1 □ 5 □ 10 □ 15 □ 20 □ 30 □ More □
Sheep?	1 □ 5 □ 10 □ 15 □ 20 □ 30 □ More □
Horses?	1 □ 5 □ 10 □ 15 □ 20 □ 30 □ More □
Windmills?	1 □ 2 □ 3 □ 4 □ 5 □ 10 □ More □
Trains?	1 □ 2 □ 3 □ 4 □ 5 □ 10 □ More □
Planes?	1 □ 2 □ 3 □ 4 □ 5 □ 10 □ More □
Who saw the first service station?	_____________________
Who saw the sea first?	_____________________
First asking to pee?	_____________________
First to say I'm hungry?	_____________________
First to say I'm thirsty?	_____________________
First to say *"Are we nearly there yet?"*	_____________________
Winner of dead lions?	_____________________

Who is in car? ______________________

____

____

Car colours:	Red □ Blue □ Green □ Yellow □
	Black □ White □ Silver □ Other □
Coaches?	1 □ 10 □ 20 □ 30 □ 40 □ 50 □ More □
Lorries?	1 □ 10 □ 20 □ 30 □ 40 □ 50 □ More □
Motor Bikes?	1 □ 10 □ 20 □ 30 □ 40 □ 50 □ More □
Caravans?	
Police Cars?	1 □ 2 □ 3 □ 4 □ 5 □ 10 □ More □
Cows?	1 □ 5 □ 10 □ 15 □ 20 □ 30 □ More □
Sheep?	1 □ 5 □ 10 □ 15 □ 20 □ 30 □ More □
Horses?	1 □ 5 □ 10 □ 15 □ 20 □ 30 □ More □
Windmills?	1 □ 2 □ 3 □ 4 □ 5 □ 10 □ More □
Trains?	1 □ 2 □ 3 □ 4 □ 5 □ 10 □ More □
Planes?	1 □ 2 □ 3 □ 4 □ 5 □ 10 □ More □
Who saw the first service station?	______________________
Who saw the sea first?	______________________
First asking to pee?	______________________
First to say I'm hungry?	______________________
First to say I'm thirsty?	______________________
First to say *"Are we nearly there yet?"*	______________________
Winner of dead lions?	______________________

Who is in car?

____

____

____

Car colours:	Red □ Blue □ Green □ Yellow □
	Black □ White □ Silver □ Other □
Coaches?	1 □ 10 □ 20 □ 30 □ 40 □ 50 □ More □
Lorries?	1 □ 10 □ 20 □ 30 □ 40 □ 50 □ More □
Motor Bikes?	1 □ 10 □ 20 □ 30 □ 40 □ 50 □ More □
Caravans?	
Police Cars?	1 □ 2 □ 3 □ 4 □ 5 □ 10 □ More □
Cows?	1 □ 5 □ 10 □ 15 □ 20 □ 30 □ More □
Sheep?	1 □ 5 □ 10 □ 15 □ 20 □ 30 □ More □
Horses?	1 □ 5 □ 10 □ 15 □ 20 □ 30 □ More □
Windmills?	1 □ 2 □ 3 □ 4 □ 5 □ 10 □ More □
Trains?	1 □ 2 □ 3 □ 4 □ 5 □ 10 □ More □
Planes?	1 □ 2 □ 3 □ 4 □ 5 □ 10 □ More □
Who saw the first service station?	___________________________
Who saw the sea first?	___________________________
First asking to pee?	___________________________
First to say I'm hungry?	___________________________
First to say I'm thirsty?	___________________________
First to say *"Are we nearly there yet?"*	___________________________
Winner of dead lions?	___________________________

9 781797 095561